AF478106

Member Hunting Camps: A Gallery

North American Outdoor Group
Minnetonka, Minnesota

Member Hunting Camps: A Gallery

Mike Vail
Vice President, Products and Business Development

Tom Carpenter
Director of Book and New Media Development

Dan Kennedy
Book Production Manager

Heather Koshiol
Book Development Coordinator

David R. Maas
Editor

Betty Lou Fegely
Cover Onlay Photo

Steve Schweitzer
Book Design and Production

ISBN 1-58159-071-7
1 2 3 4 5 / 02 01 00 99

Note: Please remember that these member stories reflect the diversity of North American Hunting Club members—both in their hunting styles as well as the regions they hunt. As different states or provinces have different regulations, please consult local laws before utilizing any of the hunting techniques suggested herein.

Contents

Introducing *Member Hunting Camps: A Gallery*

Come on a tour of some very special places.

North American Hunting Club members love their deer hunting, that's for sure. Articles in *North American Hunter*, NAHC deer hunting books and videos, NAH television shows ... it all gets devoured in our never-ending quest to become even better hunters.

But one very important aspect of deer hunting doesn't get quite as much press as controlling your scent, hunting the pre-rut period, patterning a big old buck, rattling antlers or using a grunt tube properly, scouting effectively, or any other of a multitude of strategies or techniques. And when you talk seriously with hunters, this other aspect almost always comes up as the main reason we keep coming back to the hunt year after year.

Surprisingly, the chance for a bigger buck (or any buck or any deer at all) does not appear to be the main factor drawing us back. So what is it? Just being there, in hunting camp, with family and friends. There is absolutely no other feeling like it on earth. Sure, you could still hunt without the history, traditions and people of hunting camp, but it just wouldn't be the same.

That's what *Member Hunting Camps: A Gallery* is all about. Here are dozens of member hunting camps, documented on paper and presented to you. You'll see fancy camps and simple camps, big ones and small ones, permanent structures and movable shelters, camps in

the snow and camps in the desert, camps on mountains and on prairies and in the woods and out in the swamp, camps for whitetails (of course) and camps for mule deer and even some for elk.

These pictures and stories will show you that where it is or what it's made of doesn't matter. What does matter is being there, in hunting camp again, living the traditions and being with people you care about and who share your love of the hunt.

So take a stroll through *Past & Present*, where you'll discover some camps with long and colorful histories. In *Leave It As You Found It*, help celebrate tent camps and other non-permanent hunting camps that can move with the game. In *Building a Dream*, you'll view some great escapes members have built—often fulfilling a lifelong dream. And in *A Family Affair*, you'll see that deer camp is some of the strongest glue possible for bonding fathers, sons, mothers, and daughters—any aspect of family—together.

Wood, brick, posts and beams, tin, tarpaper, plastic, canvas, nylon, even a retired camper parked in the woods ... hunting camps are built of many materials. But the most important things, the ones that last the longest, are the memories that hunting camp creates, and the good feelings it makes inside you all year long when times are a little tough and you can think back—and ahead—to hunting camp.

1940

CHAPTER one

Past & Present

Some deer camps change little over the decades. Sure, hunting party members may change slightly from year to year, but the physical structure itself—walls, roof, floor, furniture—remain relatively constant. But many deer camps are nothing like they were when the camp was founded. From additional rooms built to accommodate a new generation of young hunters, to fancy deer chalets constructed in place of old tar-paper shacks, these particular deer camps evolve through time. The camps included in this chapter celebrate both sides of this deer camp coin. The common thread—the love of the hunt and the companionship of family and friends—lives on forever, no matter how old or new the walls.

Big Bear Camp

Joe Stradel
Wayside, WI

Grandpa Joe started hunting whitetails in 1923. This was a big hunt for a 16-year-old who had to ride a train 150 miles into the Wisconsin north. Some warned Grandpa never to hunt that deep into the woods because the remote wilderness was "hell country" and he would never come out alive. He hunted there anyway, bagging trophy whitetails but never revealing his secret.

When a tiny lumberjack shack was put up for sale in 1946, Grandpa immediately purchased it. It was nothing fancy, but its location 2 miles off the main road made it the perfect place to hunt big whitetail bucks. He originally called the camp "Tipperary," after the World War II song "It's A Long, Long Way to Tipperary." Then, in 1958, they changed the name to "Big Bear Camp," after my dad, Jay, shot the state record black bear.

Throughout the years and the generations, we at Big Bear Camp have all learned that deer camp brings a little of heaven down to earth. Whether that be the stillness of a bitter cold morning on stand, or the camaraderie and stories inside the shack.

Grandpa has since passed away. Now Dad, my two brothers Jeff and Jon, and I enjoy deer camp. Soon we will add my nieces and nephews as the tradition continues.

Family bonds are tightened, appreciation for nature is strengthened, and we all come a little closer to God at Big Bear Camp. 🌲

The Old & the New

Howard Humphrey
Keene, NH

Our old deer camp was built in the 1950s with wood heat and a wood cook stove. We had kerosene lamps, no indoor plumbing, roof leaks, no insulation in the walls and water from a dug well (excellent water).

We built the new deer camp in 1989 with wood heat and a gas cookstove. We installed gas lights and a new two-seater. We insulated camp and continue to drink the same well water.

Location is West Fairlee, Vermont, on a main corridor snow machine trail. Excellent deer hunting. The camp is enjoyed year 'round by family and friends.

Grouse Land

Richard Bruce Colton
Bentonville, VA

This camp has been in existence since the 1960s. It is called "Grouse Land" for the number of grouse hunted there along with deer, bear, turkey and small game.

It is owned by John Smith Baldwin on property that has been in his family for over 100 years. Mr. Baldwin is 80 years young and a veteran of World War II and, without a doubt, one of the best Americans ever to live.

The cabin is located in Warren County, Virginia, in the Shenandoah Valley and at the foothills of the Blue Ridge Mountains.

This cabin started as a sawmill shack and has grown to its present size over the years.

Opening Day

C.J. Miller
Coloma, MI

The temperature stands at 20 degrees,
The frost clings to the forest trees,
The autumn leaves, by day yellow and red,
Are covered with crystals of white instead.

All's quiet behind the cabin door,
Except for an occasional snore,
From the hunters therein who seek the deer,
That lives in these woods throughout the year.

A restless sleep for most they say,
Because tomorrow is Opening Day.
Some dream of that buck with the "rockin' chair,"
But they may settle for one with only a pair.

"It's daylight in the swamp," someone shouts,
and the hunters start getting up and about.
Breakfast is made and they all eat their fill,
They'll need it for energy to ward off the chill.

Each prepares for the hunt in his own way,
And wishes his friends "good luck" on this day.
As each leaves the cabin with gun in his hands,
They go separate ways as they go to their stands.

A flashlight shows the hunter's way,
For the woods are still dark on this Opening Day.
He tries to tread lightly so he won't scare the deer,
But the frozen snow's crunch can be heard far and near.

As he waits on his stand for dawn's early light,
The hand on his gun is getting frostbite.
In the frosty darkness of the woods he can hear,
The sounds of the footsteps of traveling deer.

The woods start to brighten from the light of the dawn;
The hunter sees a doe and her midsummer's fawn.
As the doe and her fawn go over the hill,
He sees other movement that gives him a thrill.

For out of the jackpines with snow on his back,
Comes a beautiful buck with a ten-point rack.
The hunter's heart pounding and his mind is full of hope,
He raises his rifle and peers through the scope.

The crosshairs are centered on a vital spot,
And the deer collapses at the sound of the shot.
The hunter moves quickly to get to his prey,
Happy, yet sad, that it died on this day.

The drag to the cabin is a ten minute tramp,
And some of the others are back at the camp.
They help hang his buck on the pole by the tree,
Where it will hang for the others to see.

That night at the cabin each man tells his tale
Of the critters he saw and the deer in the swale.
Tomorrow they will head for their stand of the day
Thinking of next year's Opening Oay.

The Big Camp Black Bear Lodge & Camp Carmel

Robert M. Wertz
Middleburg, PA
Life Member

These are my two camps located near Oxboro, Maine. (This town is so small it only has a post office and no stores and everyone waves at you. It's not like anywhere I have lived.) The Big Camp Black Bear Lodge has 3 bedrooms, a full kitchen and large living room. There's no electricity, but we have a well with a hand pump and LP lights and a fridge.

The small camp is Camp Carmel. It has a kitchen and bunkroom. Both camps sit on 10 acres of land, and I own an additional 15 acres.

I've been told by some locals that Teddy Roosevelt hunted this area. Trophy whitetails, bear, moose, bobcats and coyote abound in this land. It's a place to go to escape the rat race. All the local people I've met are very friendly. There are bogs and some really big pine on my land. It's very thick and breathtaking wilderness. This is my escape.

Camp Carmel (above) and Big Camp Black Bear Lodge (right).

Chopper-Box-Turned-Deer-Camp

Jim Trotzer
Hampton, NH

Sometime in the late 1970s, my father, Roger Trotzer, abandoned an old chopper box on the edge of the woods that is our family hunting grounds in Marathon County, Wisconsin. The woods—two 40s that are part of a larger woodland and swamp area that provide excellent habitat for white-tailed deer—borders the hay- and cornfields of the farm. When my dad retired from farming and sold the farm in 1984, he kept the woodland for forest conservation and hunting purposes. The chopper box became a leftover relic from his farming days. Gerry Rhyner, one of my Dad's hunting buddies, would use the chopper box as his stand since it was located

where several excellent runways from the surrounding fields entered the woods. He always saw deer—notice I said *saw*, not *shot*. He would often explain that his lack of success was due to the cold weather and that if we would only put a stove in the chopper box to keep him warm, he would be more successful. For several years we ignored his suggestion using RVs and trailers pulled into the woods to serve as our hunting camp.

But in 1987 we finally decided to put the chopper box to use. We put an old wood burning laundry stove in it; insulated, rain/snow-proofed and refurbished it; closed in the front with cellophane; and framed in a door. We have used the chopper box as our hunting camp ever since. It has extended the hunting life of the "Old Farts" in our hunting party, like my dad and Eddie Kraft, who hang around the stove telling lies while us younger guys range far and wide in pursuit of that proverbial "tirty-pointer." And where do you think the deer show up? You guessed it. Seems like the deer prefer the chopper box too.

Camp Rip Snort

David Robinson
Latrobe, PA
Life Member

Camp Rip Snort is located in the mountains of McKean County, Pennsylvania, and was given to me in 1997 by my wife's uncle and my friend, Alfred "Bud" Everett in exchange for 1 dollar, which I never gave him.

The original camp was built around 1950 out of white oak by Bill "Wash Tubs" Zetner, Ed "Hoople" Bocz and other coal miners from Lucernemines, Pennsylvania. Harold "Pap" and Edna Everett acquired the camp around 1960. It was not until 1963 or 1964 that Bud and Pap Everett installed electricity and, with "hands on" fine-tuning and remodeling, brought the camp to its present look (years of work).

I became a frequent visitor in 1991 and harvested my first buck and first spring gobbler there with Bud as my guide. In 1997, the yearly rent on the land was raised from $30 to $720. That increase, and increasing demands on Bud's time with an aging father, now 88 years old, prompted Bud to make a change. I recruited 4 of my friends as Camp Rip Snort members: Dave Quidetto, Todd Kellerman, Mike Quidetto and Wally Zeunges. We all share the expenses and upkeep. The camp now boasts a propane heating system, updated carpeting, a kitchen and a heated outhouse.

In addition to our traditional hunting seasons—deer, bear, turkey—we share the camp with families. Activities include telling campfire stories and long dragged-out hunting stories, roasting marshmallows, catching native brook trout and crayfish or just splashing in nearby 5 or 7 Mile Run with my kids. The kids enjoy swimming at nearby Bendigo State Park and fishing in East Branch Lake at Elk State Park, visiting beaver dams and taking long walks in the woods.

Throughout our 6 years of hunting together, Bud would frequently exclaim "Holy Rip Snort!" when he was excited or surprised. In his honor I named the camp "Camp Rip Snort." 🌲

Camp Bucktail

Thomas McWherter
Derry, PA
Life Member

Camp Bucktail is located in St. Mary's, Elk County, Pennsylvania. It has been in constant use since 1944, when eight hardy souls, led by George Kuhns, erected the first small cabin on the property. The cabin has been greatly expanded since that time. George is the only original member still active in the camp.

Buck season is, of course, the most active of the year. Anywhere from 12 to 24 men and boys of all ages gather to hunt the elusive trophy. Stories are told. Old successes and failures are relived. And everyone rejoices when a buck is brought in and hauled up on the hanging pole. Most importantly, the traditions of the camp and hunting are passed from old to young.

Although deer hunting is the primary purpose of the camp, we hunt bear, turkey, grouse, rabbits and squirrels. Sometimes we even do some trout fish-

ing in the area's icy trout streams. There are times when members and guests gather to enjoy the camp in other ways: playing golf on the scenic mountain courses in the area, just reading, taking scouting walks in the forest and, of course, appreciating the ever-present joy of other members. Our only concession to modern conveniences is that the camp has electricity but no running water, and we heat the cabin with a wood stove. We gather in May of each year to perform maintenance on the camp and to chop wood for the upcoming hunting season.

The only rules we have for the camp are:

What goes on at camp stays at camp.
(Mothers do try to pump their young sons for juicy details.)

You can do anything you want at camp.
(Sort of goes with rule 1.)

No women during hunting season.
(Sorry ladies, but you are welcome at other times.)

We are very lucky to have a place like Camp Bucktail to enjoy the good things of nature.

No Mortgage

Arthur A. Sechrist
Fleetwood, PA

Deer camp location: Tuscorora State Forest, Perry County, Pennsylvania.
Owner: Arthur A. Sechrist.
Cabin size: 16 feet x 22 feet and attached to a wood shed.
Built: Early 1920s.
Construction: Chestnut logs and hand-split cedar shake roof.
Facilities: LP gas lights, 2 burner hot plate, wood stove heat, sleeps 4, outside composting toilet, spring water about 75 yards distant, hot plate, dutch oven, reflector oven and outside fireplace for mild weather use. No electricity, no phone, no TV, no mortgage. 🌲

Montana Café

Bill and Mike Latta
Stilwell, OK

After spending a full 9-day rainy deer season camping in a small pop-up trailer one year, we decided that we probably had enough lumber just lying around to build a small cabin. The first year it was 10' x 10' with a metal roof. To us—fantastic!

With help from our hunting buddies Sam Lasiter and Calvin Carson, and our sons (six total), it's now 20' x 20'. The cabin sleeps 10 people, has a cooking area and sitting room where we all tell "the-one-that-got-away" stories.

Though it sits in the hills of Oklahoma green country, we named it "Montana Café," because its specialty is peace of mind.

A Silver Anniversary for Oakridge

Bill Buckman
Bogata, TX

For 2 hours, the deep narrow opening in the thick brushy terrain has been void of movement. Now at dusky dark some 100 yards near the far end of this cleared strip, a slight movement catches my attention. I can faintly make out the presence of a deer camouflaged to the leafy floor background. A single deer broadside in the cut has often proven to be a buck, so I raise my 10x50s for a view.

Bingo! The rack is partially covered from overhang, but I quickly make out his beams sweeping to his ear tips in length. I can't identify tines, but I can certainly see that the buck is looking straight uphill in my direction. I assume he is gazing directly at me, so I expect him to bolt from my slightest movement. With the utmost caution, I proceed to lower the optics and reach for the XL-H .356 Win. single shot handgun on a shelf to my right. Surprisingly, the deer remains motionless as I lay this precision piece across the front gun support of my large box blind. Just as I field him in the 4X

Leupold scope, he slowly turns to quarter away. Since he is going up the hill, a lot of target is revealed. I steady to the shot as the big boomer jumps from its heavy recoil. The buck disappears into thick underbrush. I wait a short time, then climb from the high stand to investigate. A trail of crimson drops and disturbed soil soon lead to the downed buck.

This nice 7-point buck is not a large deer of rack or body; however, he is not just another whitetail buck. He is #25 out of 25 years on this lease and #20 in the last 20 years at this very spot taken with a handgun. He is a historic buck to me.

I am proud of most bucks that I take, but this one is different. This deer was a goal in my life as a deer hunter. Like the chimes of a grandfather clock alerting me to the hour, this buck reminds me not only of my age, but also of what my hunting camp means to me. It causes me to reminisce about 3 decades of deer hunting, especially the last 25 years.

I began taking white-tailed deer hunting seriously in 1968. I was fresh out of college and had a good job, a new wife, and a new home. And, thanks to a Detroit, Texas, gunsmith, I had a new rifle. My first buck on a cold November morning in 1969 was the start of my long-held obsession for deer. That dandy 7-point buck still hangs in my reloading room to remind me of that red-letter day.

Of all the deer leases and hunts I've experienced (and there have been several), one place stands out above all the others. It's known as Oakridge Hunting Club (est. 1962). In 1972, with help from dear friends, I became the newest member of this historic deer lease located about 40 miles from my home in the northeast corner of Red River County, Texas. The camp house is nestled on a ridge of majestic oak trees not far from the Red River near good upland and bottomland timber of pine and hardwood. Remotely confined a good mile from the nearest county dirt road, Oakridge was one of the best of all local camps. It had even been written about in the magazine of the Dallas Times Herald.

Deer stands were numerous in my early days at the camp, but most were not very elaborate. With the addition of younger members, the stands became much more plush with tops and sides. Many stands were built on poles and were no longer just a board nailed in a tree. Comfortable blinds became the norm. We even built a few of these swanky "hotels" for some of the more dedicated older members.

I've remained at the same spot for the last 20 years, always hunting with a big-bore handgun. I've dolled-up my tall pole stand as it has developed needs. Shooting rests have been incorporated for handgunning. As I became more skilled, longer lanes and openings became maintained for my shooting. The stand is where I spend many hours writing and reading, so it's kept comfortable. There is one drawback: Buzzards seem to like my winter roost in the summer. Looking on the bright side, at least the stinking carnivores do offer camouflaging odor in the fall.

Back in '72, the cabin had no electricity, but it had good gas lights and appliances—of course, a potbelly wood heater. Membership was near 15 men of mixed ages. Many were old timers who didn't hunt hard anymore, but were they ever full of hmmm ... shall we say, interesting tales. We younger ones often thought them lazy, but now I understand that they were wise in the philosophy of, "Why should we do things that the younger ones can do better?"

In 1963, the cabin building was moved some 40 miles from Fulbright, Texas, where it had served as a community center for many years. The move to this beautiful location and conversion to a hunting camp seem to breathe new life into the old building. Other than a little renovation after the original move, it has been kept much the same, although we have added a big front porch along with electricity via power generator. We also built a hanging room, but it soon got converted to storage and a 4-wheeler garage. The cabin has maintained its original structure of 2 rooms. The kitchen is complete with a large eating table, gas refrigerator, stove and a large café grill. Adjacent is one large room of easy chairs, a wood stove and a domino table where many a heated game has evolved. At the opposite end of the large room are 6 double bunks. With only 8 members now, the top bunks usually serve as storage for gear.

The decor has probably gone through the biggest change. The number of racks that adorn the walls, rafters, and porch posts continues to grow. The cook, Charley, has his racks mounted in one end of "his" kitchen. (Including his 7-point doe.) Walls of the big room are covered with pictures and posters galore. There are Bud girls, Coors girls, Winchester twins, and about fifteen years of Buck Stop Bambies. Many are personally autographed, "To the guys at Oakridge." (Susan K.—Playboy's Miss January '77 would be proud.) It's a hunter's paradise.

I've seen a lot of changes in timber cover on the lease since that first hunting day in that little treestand located 200 yards below the john. The devastating Paris tornado of '82 tore its way along our southern border, leaving unusual landmarks. Sheet metal from nearby barns and chicken houses still grace much of the landscape. Then about 9 years ago, loggers wiped out the hardwood and most of the pine; however, they did leave a number of pines for seeding in my area. The twister's debris became just unusual landmarks, but the logging brought a drastic change in hunting. We continued to keep the roads open the best we could around the cut timber piles and skidder ruts. It's paying off now as we have good trails in the regrowth. Oddly, the deer often maintain many of the same routes even though the canopy of large trees is gone. Deer movement and numbers seem to be picking back up now. We plant food plots and supplement feed through stress periods; plus, we add salt and mineral in the summer. We learn to do what we have to do to maintain a decent deer population. Unfortunately, timber cutting of the remaining seed trees is probably planned for the not-too-distant future.

In 25 years, there have been sad moments. Many of the old timers have passed on to the great deer camp in the sky. Members like our leader and founder L.B. have been gone for several years. We often speak of him and miss his orneriness and his humor. We learned a lot from those who have gone to the Happy Hunting Grounds.

Fortunately, joyous moments outnumber those of sadness. Like those happy days when you got your buck or maybe the time you spotted Mr. Mossback. They're not to be forgotten. Or that year your best friend or son became a member and got his first deer. Charlie's son, Charles Don, got his first deer here, then his second and third. Suddenly he wasn't a kid anymore. In what seemed like a blink of an eye, he's a grown man with a wife, a child, and one on the way. Our roles have reversed, too. Charles Don is our youth now, and we're the old timers wanting to be waited on. Life really is a circle.

Oakridge has been our home away from home, and we grew up in a special way here. Modern conveniences such as the 4-wheeler hint that nothing is very remote anymore. Although we seldom see a really big buck due to all the hunting pressure around, we do see bucks. But that's not it entirely. Oakridge is more than the quantity or quality of its deer. Oakridge is tradition and comradeship. The feeling that exists between its members cannot be found just anywhere, nor can it be explained to outsiders.

It was dark when I arrived back at camp with 'ole #25. There were only 4 of us that night. We celebrated with fried venison and fried squirrels and all the trimmings—mashed potatoes, sawmill butter (gravy), peas, corn and biscuits. As usual, we then turned to storytelling over a few games of 42. We stayed up a little later than usual that night, turning in around 10:30. (We're getting older, you know.) Then too, there were a couple of fellows who still had some hunting to do early the next morning.

Although I had my buck for the county quota, I still enjoy going to the stand to read, to write and to observe the wildlife. Just taking it easy enjoying the environment and being thankful to our Maker. That's what Oakridge Hunting Club is all about. Enjoyment and relaxation. Doing what you like to do. A good place to celebrate a 25th anniversary.

"Charles Don, how about getting me a pop out of the cooler? Cheers. And happy hunting ..."

Mapleton Hunting Camp

Tom Cramer
Mapleton, PA

The Mapleton Hunting Camp was formed on December 25, 1924, at Baker's Barber Shop in Mapleton, Pennsylvania. The original 18 members were all from Mapleton. There were a lot of improvements made on the "old camp" through the years. A kitchen and a porch were added in the earlier years. Later there was an upstairs added with the "quiet room."

The "old camp" burned down in November 1984. It was the first Thursday of buck season. The cause of the fire is still unknown.

The "new camp" was built in the summer of 1985. The building is 30' x 40', heated with oil forced air and sleeps 30. There are no interior walls upstairs or downstairs. The kitchen, dining room and living room are on the first floor. The sleeping area and shower are on the second floor. A heated outhouse is several feet from the front door.

There are presently 42 members of the Mapleton hunting camp, which is located in Union Township in Huntingdon County, Pennsylvania. It is next to the State Game Lands where the members enjoy hunting various small game, turkeys and white-tailed deer.

The Ogema Tornado

Nicky Michels
Port Edwards, WI

In 1995 we purchased 75 acres of land in Ogema, Wisconsin. We built a 24' x 24' cabin on a concrete slab; after many long hours and miles, we had a fully finished hunting cabin. With 2 weeks left before opening day of bow season, we now had time to relax. Three days later, my brother-in-law, James Schuerman, and I were at our fire department having a meeting with other members and the weather was on television. They were saying that Ogema was getting hit hard with hail. Well, right away the guys were riding us about having to redo our roof. Five minutes later my wife walked in the door and called me off to the side. She said our neighbor from up north had just called and told us a tornado just went through, and we no longer had a hunting cabin. Nobody was hurt—although 30 yards from the cabin a fine 6-point lay dead—and we did have the cabin insured.

Our new cabin we built is a 22' x 28' A-frame with a full basement. We are now finished with our cabin and have installed a basketball hoop up where our first cabin was. 🌲

*Above: Our newly-built cabin before the tornado.
Right: The current cabin during deer season.*

County Line Camp

Joseph M. Inglese
Amsterdam, NY

The camp I belong to is in the Adirondack Mountains of New York. It is in Hamilton County in the town of Wells. Our camp is unique in that it is coming up on its 77th anniversary.

The camp was started in 1922 by a group of men from Amsterdam, New York. Previous to that, the camp was home to a Civil War veteran. He had the building moved to its current location from a lumbering/tanning town called Griffin some 3 miles away. (Griffin no longer exists.) We hold title and deed to the camp and land directly from the Civil War veteran. In our region, most camps are situated on leases from the big paper companies. The members on such leases hold no real ownership.

We are proud of our historical significance and that the founders set down by-laws that have helped keep the camp intact all these years. The camp is called the County Line Camp because it is located along New York State Highway 8, not far from the Hamilton/Warren County line. 🌲

Buck Camp: Poker Camp

William E. Duncan
Cedarville, CA
Life Member

This buck camp, probably like many, had a somewhat innocuous beginning, explained thusly: Its birth came about not so much as needed shelter for hunters (which of course is what it is), but because of the love of a friendly game of poker. As "Two Bit" 7-card stud became the norm at the close of the hunting day, backs of pickup trucks and small tents were not adequate to accommodate all the participants.

So one year I brought a ¾" 4' x 8' sheet of plywood, several posts, and some planking for benches. Four of these posts were sunk 3 feet in the ground and framed, and the plywood was attached to the top. Posts were sunk in the ground for the benches, and we had a permanent table capable of seating 10 or 12 hunters/poker players. And thence the beginning of a permanent "buck camp."

Being in a somewhat windy area, we often found ourselves chasing cards blown from the table and, for poker players, this can be very annoying. Four poles were erected around the table, and tarps were hung between them for whichever way the wind was blowing. This helped some, but in the erratic winds, we found that the tarps had to be moved often and in stronger winds, the tarps shredded. So the next year, wood walls were erected around the

table and a metal roof was constructed to ward off the rain and snow that would interfere with the game. For the next several years, other improvements came about: a door was installed, windows installed, a bunk room to sleep 5, a storage room, wood heat stove, propane lights, refrigerator, cookstove, outdoor shower, outhouse, and more.

And even though there is no running water, no electricity and, best of all, no telephones, it's a great place to be.

Invitations, confined to family and very long-time hunting partners, needless to say are very cherished, and rank with a one-on-one audience with the Pope or sideline seats at the Super Bowl. Weddings, births, funerals, birthdays and anniversaries have all been missed because of invitations to "buck camp."

Like most "buck camps," traditions seem to evolve: Here are a few of ours:

- One of the earliest was no women (this has been revised over the years)
- First buck killed, "chops" are consumed by the others
- Newest and youngest hunters select their preferred hunting areas
- First in camp opens and cleans camp
- Last out closes camp
- All straight flushes in the poker games are labeled and tacked on the wall (a whole wall is nearly full)
- No alcohol until all hunters are in camp and guns are safely retired
- No discussions of jobs or business is permitted
- Angry or cross words are not permitted in "buck camp"
- Any jokes, posters, notes, etc. attached to the wall by any hunter in camp, cannot be removed by another
- Any monies dropped from the table during a poker game cannot be picked up by anyone (dirt floor)
- If any hunter needs help, becomes lost, stuck or whatever, all hunters must assist in a rescue
- Each year in the fall, since its erection, the laughter and merriment echoing its walls cannot be equaled
- Although this camp has a 90% success rate with many trophy-sized bucks taken, Buck Camp's origin must be credited to poker

The Susquehannock Club

Joe Spaltro
Placitas, NM

The Susquehannock Club in Potter County, Pennsylvania, was established around 1938 by World War I veterans from American Legion Post
#27 in Harrisburg. They purchased a log cabin on 100 acres with a stretch of
trout stream. Membership has passed from the founders through their relatives, friends, friends of friends and some of their descendants. One of the
founders, Col. Roy Taylor, was a key man in the formation of the Women's
Army Corp (WAC's) in WW II.

As per the property deed and local scuttlebutt, the cabin began life in the 1920s as a most isolated retreat for the alcoholic son of a Wellesboro, Pennsylvania, physician. The cabin has a complete kitchen and bath and can sleep 20 … in beds! No phone. No TV. Minimal, poor radio reception.

Notwithstanding all the deer, bear, turkey and woodchuck hunting, trout fishing, and shooting activities, the principal theme of the club has always been toward getaways for families and friends. It has been the place where many kids (including some of the now-senior members) have learned to enjoy and respect nature, trout hooks and firearms. Every visit and meeting has been recorded in logs dating back to 1947. This wonderful history traces the club's evolution, with additions and losses. The entries vary from the severely laconic to humorous verbosity. Accompanying photo albums enhance the logbooks' appeal.

The current membership of 19 (maximum 20) mostly reside in Pennsylvania, with some scattered into New Jersey, New York, Maryland, Vermont and New Mexico. It includes several veterans, 2 state troopers, a few graduate degree-holders and a long-standing honorary member: the now-retired sheriff of Potter County. 🌲

Lincoln Log

Tad E. Crawford
East Sparta, OH

How about this for a really neat hunt camp? I own 122 acres, mostly wooded (a great white oak woods) with a few acres of food plot. The farm is one of the highest elevations overlooking Tappan Lake in Harrison County, Ohio. We've killed lots of nice deer there including 2 that just missed Boone & Crockett Club (by approximately ⅛ inch!) and a few in the 140s and 150s. The cabin, is pre-Civil War, so I named it the Lincoln Log.

Built before the time of Abe Lincoln, it is an original dovetail log, stands on its original site and has yielded a newspaper printed during the Civil War and even a family Bible from that era! It has unlimited free natural gas from a gas well on the property so I heat it all year. It has air conditioning, a gas log fireplace (also backup electric hydronic baseboard heaters), a great water well and a couple of small fish ponds. I have seen lots of turkey, squirrel, deer and the odd black bear. Being off the main road about a mile gives lots of privacy.

The sad news though, is that most of my old hunting buddies have gone or are too feeble to hunt. A few years back I fell from a treestand, breaking my back and foot, so I hardly hunt here anymore. Keeping up with this place and my other home has become a bit much, so I guess I'll just have to sell it.

Revived Hunting Camp

Jasper Hatch
Dexter, ME

This old hunting camp was built in the Maine woods for white-tailed deer in the early 1960s by John Day and his brother Lou Day.

Years had gone by and it was falling down when Peter Payne and I, brought it back to life in 1998.

Green Mill Cabin

Robert Luke Martin
Clinton, IN

The center section of the cabin was built in the 1930s for a saw mill group. In 1992 we added two rooms for bedrooms. All of it is built with green mill lumber. We use it for turkey and deer seasons and sometimes to relax and enjoy the peacefulness of the woods.

Located in west central Indiana, it has no running water or electricity and an outside john.

Four old retired hunters and 2 "young bucks" use the cabin. We heat with wood and cook with LP gas.

Sporting Hill Rod & Gun Club

Lester Weidman
Manheim, PA

Location: Lycoming County, Pennsylvania.

Name of camp: Sporting Hill Rod and Gun Club.

History: The camp was built in the early 1920s by 16 men who lived in Sporting Hill, Lancaster County, Pennsylvania. One of the 16 was my grandfather, Elmer Weidman. The camp remains in the family today. Numerous whitetail bucks, 2 black bear and a few turkey have been taken over the years. The camp is also used as a vacation spot for members and guests.

Traditions: A buck kitty is formed every year for the person getting the first buck. Rum cake is served at our first meal, even though we are a dry camp.

Pine Swamp Gun Club

Robert Moyer
Pottsville, PA

The Pine Swamp Gun Club is located outside of Summit Station in Schuylkill County, Pennsylvania. The original camp was built in the 1930s. This is the third building built by the membership since that time. Our present building was built in 1974. We own 9¾ acres and have access to stated game lands that border our property on 3 sides.

We have a current membership of 18 with a full membership set at 25. Most members are from Schuylkill County, and the ones from outside the area grew up with fathers and relatives belonging to camp. About half the members are second and third generations of camp. The cabin sleeps 23, has hot and cold water and gas and electric lights from a generator. Water is a gravity fee system to camp from a creek running through the property.

Since 1974 we have had only 2 years when no deer were taken. We have had black bear, coyotes, and many turkeys at and around camp. Besides using the camp for hunting, members use it for weekend getaways and get togethers. Meetings are the second Sundays from March to December.

The Former Slaughterhouse

Thomas B. Cramer
Sewell, NJ

Our deer camp is in Sherman Mills, Maine. In the early 1900s, it was actually a slaughterhouse for local area residents. There is no running water and no modern heat,

but we do have electricity. I have enclosed a before and an after picture.

We spend a lot of time telling stories of the day's hunt outside at the burning barrel. The deer in the area do not come by in quantity, but they make up for it with quality.

We have 4 hunters in camp with the name of Tom, 1 Todd, and 1 Ronney. It is great to spend some quality men time with these fellows each deer season, no matter if we get meat for the freezer or not.

Our Swamp

Ken Nernberger
Medford, WI

This is "Our Swamp." We spent 17 years moving this 19-foot trailer around and deer hunting from it. Three years ago we purchased 5 acres of land and added an 8- x 12-foot addition.

In 1998, we built this 24- x 28-foot cabin, which is a great improvement. The owners are Al Higgins, Gary Frischman, Lynn Nernberger, Peter Degraves and Ken Nernberger.

Above: the old trailer.
Right: the new cabin.

Jacob's Cabin

Chris MacCartney
Mentor, OH

This is our family hunting camp in the Upper Peninsula of Michigan. My great grandfather Jacob built the camp. The smaller of the 2 cabins (on the left) was built in 1930 and the larger building was built in 1932. The two cabins were originally further apart than they are today. The smaller cabin was rolled over closer to the big cabin using horses and trees to roll it on. The walkway between the two was built shortly thereafter.

My grandfather taught me about hunting and nature through spending time at the cabin. From appreciating nature for what it was to learning how to shoot my first rifle, my grandfather taught me a lot. My brothers and I learned and are still learning what the meaning of hard work is. There is no electricity and the running water we do have was built out of a handmade dam.

One of the most important lessons I have learned from Grandpa is not to head out into the woods without a compass. The area where we hunt up there is very dense. You're lucky to get a 50-yard shot and it's very easy to get turned around. I have heard many stories where hunting buddies have gotten lost and they had to go find them.

My great grandfather, my grandfather, my dad, my brothers and I have all enjoyed hunting and fishing from our second home. Hopefully I can pass this on to my children.

Newport Rod & Gun Club

Ed Gebhart
Carlisle, PA

Our camp is located in Mifflin County, Pennsylvania, in Treaster Valley. Organized in 1920, the camp sits on state ground that we lease. The cabin will sleep 18 people upstairs and is lit by gas lights both upstairs and down. We have running water that is gravity fed from a stream in the hollow above camp. We have hot and cold running water, our kitchen has a cookstove plus a gas stove. We also have a gas water heater in the kitchen. Our dining and living area is located off of the kitchen. Heat is supplied by a potbelly stove and a fireplace. If you want to take a shower we hook a hose to the kitchen faucet and run this out the window—you shower outside.

There are currently 23 members in camp. The camp is open for use by family members except during hunting seasons when it is open to all members. We have a work-party weekend when repairs are done around camp. Pranks are pulled by a few camp members like putting toads in your sleeping bag or hiding a 3" pvc pipe lengthwise under your mattress. They have even put metal bands around 2 members' beds.

Our camp cook, Les, feeds us quite well. If you go away from camp hungry, it's your fault. Also, meals are served on time—if you're late you take a chance of not eating. One member has a lucky fishing rod he uses. The only guide on it is the one at the tip. He does catch some big trout using only a hook with a piece of red cloth on it. We've also had a pig roast at camp.

Our guys are a good group who get along well and get things done. We hope our camp is around for years to come. If you ever get by our camp stop to see if Dave is there; I'm sure he will show you his fishing rod. Also Les might let you sample his good cooking. But watch out for those guys who pull pranks because they might get you too! To become a member you have to hunt and attend work parties before you can be voted in. 🌲

Vintage Hunting Camp

Darrell Hoeft
Watertown, WI

Here is our deer camp. We built it in 1943 and have hunted the entire time.

We started with about 9 hunters, and it has stayed about the same. The older hunters have died off and there now are about 6 or 7 left. I hunted from 1946 until 4 years ago. We have all county land around us and they clear cut it all and now it has to grow up. I have personally taken 56 whitetails from the cabin as good as I can count. It has been a good hunting spot for over 53 years, and the deer will surely come back very soon. ♠

Memories

Willard Garis
Souderton, PA

These are not pictures! They are memories: memories of how life has changed and memories of how enjoyable life can be. Memories of a shack and how it has changed over the years—43 years to be exact.

In the old days, the only way to get to deer camp was by backpacking or hiring a logger and his team of horses with wagon and sled. In 1955, we paid Vern $12 to haul our supplies into camp. In 1958 we hired Phil and his team of horses, which cost $15 for a day.

Early on there were five of us brothers. Later, in 1970, the first of our sons made the trip. In the early '70s, the lean-to on the left side of the camp was removed, and a larger "A" roof addition was built. Later that decade, in 1978, the lumbering company built the first new roads near our camp, which allowed us to drive 4-wheel-drive trucks close

(several hundred yards) to camp. It's a good thing too; those toters were getting harder to push each year!

Sometime during the summer of 1984, someone attempted to burn down the camp. The fire burned itself out before the camp burned down. By the following hunting season, though, we had built our camp back up.

My grandson's first Maine hunt took place in 1997. That year three generations of Garis's shared the experience of a lifetime. Father, son and grandson all got nice bucks. Pictured (below) are my brother Richard,

son Jay (10-point buck), myself (7-point buck), my grandson Duane (8-point buck) and brother Russell, who died in 1998. That season is one of the best memories of my life.

Aime's Cabin

Glenn Pilling
Spiritwood, Saskatchewan, Canada

This is our Deer/Moose camp in the Canadian North. We will be celebrating the 25th anniversary of our group hunting the area of the camp. The week each fall we spend at hunting camp is usually the only time we get together to tell lies, renew friendships, and do a little hunting.

Our camp is located in a large tract of forest that covers approximately 600 square miles. It is over 20 miles from the nearest road, so we rarely see other hunters. The camp was originally started by a trapper in 1947.

We have kept good records since we began hunting the area, and up to last season we have taken 47 whitetail bucks and 32 moose from the camp.

We feel extremely fortunate to have such a beautiful place to hunt and enjoy old friends.

Cedar Grove Camp

Peter Christensen
Dartmouth, Nova Scotia, Canada

Cedar Grove Camp is located in Maple Grove, Hants County, Nova Scotia, Canada. Originally built in 1958 by my father, Neil Christensen, and his best friend, Charlie Dolliver, Cedar Grove Camp was built in an old abandoned farm field. It is located approximately one mile off a secondary highway. The homesteaders planted a row of cedar trees along the edge of the field. Cedar trees are not plentiful in this area; therefore, the camp received the name Cedar Grove Camp. In addition, the homesteaders must have planted a horseshoe chestnut tree which is also unique to the area.

I have been hunting out of Cedar Grove Camp all my life. Other friends have become regulars at the camp. My sons are now hunting from Cedar Grove Camp. Other members of the camp are Ron Jean, Steve Watson, Fred Kent, Kendell Kent, James Spruin and Tom Manton.

Unfortunately, the camp burned to the ground in the summer of 1987. Some local children had gotten into the camp and the fire was started accidentally. Up to that time, we leased the property from a local landowner. After the fire, I was successful in purchasing the property with the intentions of building a new camp. Since there were only 8 weeks until the opening of the whitetail season, a concentrated effort was made to rebuild the camp. The camp was successfully completed the weekend before opening day.

As with most deer camps, we share a great camaraderie, a lot of good times, card games, food and spirits. Charlie Dolliver, who was a very skilled deer hunter, passed away in 1989. Charlie always appreciated the size and weight of a deer over its antlers. He took many fine bucks and we now have a trophy in his honor. Another tradition at our camp is to hang the deer in the chestnut tree in front of the camp. The Charlie Dolliver Memorial Trophy is awarded annually to the hunter who had the heaviest deer hanging in the tree. Some of our members have yet to win the trophy. There is friendly competition for this trophy every fall. I am very proud to have won the trophy four times since 1989. Kendell Kent has won the trophy on 3 occasions.

Originally the members at the Cedar Grove Camp were all rifle hunters, but many of us now have taken up bowhunting. We have taken several large deer with both bow and rifle. I have included a few photographs for your enjoyment.

The original hunters at the camp were all still-hunters, which is how many of the present members learned to deer hunt. We continue to still-hunt, but we also stand hunt. Many of our stands have been placed in areas where we have been successful with our still-hunting. In fact, many of our better stands have names such as Peter's Hardwood Hill, The Burns Farm Stand, The Hardwood Ridge, The Intersection, The Well Road Stand, and The Bernie Clancy (there is a story behind that name).

We still enjoy an abundance of places to hunt, and we hunt both private

and Crown land. The bag limit for white-tailed deer is 1 antler deer with visible antlers of at least 3 inches. There is also a doe draw for various zones throughout the province.

We have a very good relationship with the local landowners and residents by being courteous and helpful to them when we can. We also maintain a good relationship with the local game warden, Mike Lowe.

We are very proud of our camp and our hunting traditions. We could probably write our own book about special hunts and experiences at Cedar Grove Camp. We have numerous photographs dating back to 1958.

Since the original hunters were mainly meat hunters, many of the large racks have been lost. We have been able to locate many of the racks, and they are displayed inside the camp. Also, we keep a shed collection. Some of the large sheds certainly give great incentive for the next hunting season.

Our bucks average 180 to 200 pounds field-dressed. There are also bucks taken in the province that weigh in excess of 250 pounds field-dressed. My largest buck, which I was fortunate enough to take with my bow, was a 10-pointer, weighing 233 pounds field-dressed.

Canton Lodge

Elmer Huiras
Rice Lake, WI

Our present building in northern Wisconsin was purchased for $50, taken down log by log, loaded on a 1½ ton Chevy truck and hauled 90 miles up north where we purchased a ½ acre lot for another $50. This was in 1958. Our group of 10 started hunting here in Bayfield County that fall,

having moved from another area and ending the tent camping of previous years. The next year the gang got together and drove a well point down 55 feet to water and put a hand pump in the cabin that still pumps our water for us. An airtight wood stove heated the cabin for years until it rusted out and was replaced by a barrel stove that is still in use. There is no electricity, so gasoline lanterns and LP lights are used along with a gas refrigerator. We added on a 16' square area for the bunk beds, so we then had much more room and a cooler sleeping room away from the stove.

In our diary we have kept the hunting experiences of every day of hunting for the last 41 years. The original books are typewritten into a large loose-leaf book with everything in one book. We also have a circulating trophy for the biggest

buck by antler each year. When you get your name on 3 years you keep the trophy and a new one is purchased. In the 41 years, we have given away only 4 trophies, so the competition is fairly even. Another plaque is on the wall with a

nameplate and the years for the hunter who had the biggest buck. An 11" x 14" enlargement of the deer kill is put on the wall each year for the record with the names of the successful hunters. The fourth generation of families is now hunting with us and 6 of the original hunters are still hunting.

51

A Brief History of Stony Brook Club, Inc.

Leon I. VanWie
Watertown, NY

In the 1870s, Frank A. Cutting, a hemlock bark dealer with headquarters in Boston, Massachusetts, with two other men, purchased 8,000 acres of virgin timber in the town of Hopkinton. The 8,000 acres later became known as the Cutting Tract and is now occupied by the Stony Brook Club, Inc. In 1882, Frank Cutting acquired full ownership.

The hemlock bark was used by Cutting in the tanning of leather. Leather shoes were made in Massachusetts and the hemlock bark produced tannic acid that was used in the tanning process. Cutting's only use of the land was for the hemlock, so he sold the pine and spruce trees to the Clark Lumber Company of Parishville sometime prior to 1900.

Throughout the early 1900s, 3 companies harvested wood from the Cutting Tract: the Brooklyn Cooperage Company harvested hardwood logs, St. Regis Paper Company cut the softwoods and Frank Cutting continued to harvest the hemlock bark.

By the 1920s, chemicals replace the tannic acid from the hemlock bark used in the tanning of leather, so Cutting sold the Tract to the Gould Paper Company on December 29, 1926. The cost to the Gould Paper Company was $23,500. Frank Cutting maintained ownership of the property around Lake Ozonia that included his summer camp. On December 22, 1929, Gould Paper Company sold the property to the formation of the Stony Brook Club; the area was virtually "open range," and the logging buildings were freely used by hunters and fisherman.

Between 1935 and 1937, there were mainly 2 groups of hunters using the Cutting Tract for hunting. A group from Massena was hunting out of the Train Pond Camp. The other group hunted out of Bull Priest's camp on Stony Brook.

Bull Priest was the bartender at the Van Heuvel Hotel in Heuvelton. Priest formulated the "Stony Brook Club" idea to establish a set of rules that would protect hunting in the future. The Massena group was concerned that Bull Priest's idea might prevent them from hunting, so a combined meeting was called. Mr. Sid Williams from the Massena group asked what would happen to the group from Train Pond. Mr. Priest's answer was that they had plenty of land for their requirements and as long as those fellows minded their own business, they would not be disturbed and maybe they could join his club. The combined group felt that if they joined together and got organized, "a great hunting club" could be formed. Sid Williams was appointed to work up a set of by-laws. Sid was a great organizer and a hard worker. Thus, the Stony Brook Club was born.

On June 27, 1939, a meeting was held in Canton for the purpose of incorporating. The incorporation papers were signed on August 15, 1939, and on August 30, 1939, the certificates were filed with New York State.

"The young men who had formed the club were a rambunctious group of farmers and other hardworking men who worked hard at relaxing." One of these "young men" was Herb Holland from DePeyster.

The original club had 60 members and the annual dues cost $80. Guest fees were $1 per day, and $6 was the initiation fee when a member first

joined. The largest waiting list was in 1968 when there were 130 waiting. The "Special Member" category began in 1964 for sons, etc. Pat (Bulger) Johnson was the first female member and was accepted in 1980. Each year the "Life Membership" grows longer, indicating that the membership is growing older.

In February 1992, George Gill became a life member and Leon VanWie became a regular member.

The History of West Line Group

The West Line Camp was built in 1938 by Herb Holland (one of the founding members of the Stony Brook Club) and his nephew Bud Rock. Herb was a farmer from DePeyster who lived about a mile from Harry Reynolds and Stan Todd. Herb was a bachelor, who built the camp primarily for his nephew, Bud. On the farm in DePeyster, Herb cut the trees and sawed the lumber to build the camp. He used an old stake rack truck to bring the lumber to Stony Brook to build the hunting camp.

During the first 2 years Herb, and Bud were about the only hunters at the West Line Camp. Around 1940 Harry Reynolds and Stan Todd began coming. Bud was killed while serving in the United States Army during World War II. George Gill started hunting out of the camp in either 1946 or 1947. Herb Holland gave the hunting camp to Harry and George. Also, there was a note in Herb's will leaving the camp to them.

Originally, Herb and Bud had used an old kerosene stove to cook on. Later on, the gas stove that is used now was brought in and it sat on top of the old kerosene stove. The gas stove has been used ever since. George built a frame to set the stove on, at which time the kerosene stove was removed.

The camp box wood stove that is used now was once used in Harry Gill's store in Antwerp.

During the early years of hunting out of the camp, those going to the West Line Camp needed to park at the gravel bed, which is located at the corner of Sylvan Falls Road and Reynolds Road, 1.3 miles from the West Line Camp. Rush Reynolds built a camp off of the main road at Sylvan Falls around 1950. Since he was the Highway Superintendent from the town of Antwerp, he built a road over to his camp. Those hunting at West Line Camp could then park at Rush Reynolds camp and walk in 9/10 mile.

The current road was built in 1983–1984 when the Champion Paper Company began logging off Stony Brook Camp.

Tom Gill began hunting out of West Line Camp in 1968 and Leon VanWie began in 1985.

The first major structural improvements to the West Line Camp were made in 1987 when the sill on the west side was replaced by George and Dick McCabe.

In 1989 George and Bob Dier jacked up the entire camp and replaced eight feet of the floor on the North end of the camp.

Throughout the years as many as 8 have hunted out of the camp on a single day. 🌲

CHAPTER two

LEAVE IT AS YOU FOUND IT

It may have been your parents who taught you respect for the outdoors. Or maybe it was a grandparent or a friend's dad or mom. No matter where or how you learned it, the rule about how to treat the natural world is simple: Leave it as you found it. Most camps featured on the following pages take this responsibility of keeping the outdoors beautiful very seriously. Thanks to these respectful hunters and others throughout North America, the chance of finding "a nice place to set up camp" has never been better.

Baldy Bunch

Dave Hall
Ellensburg, WA

Our hunting camp is tucked into the side of Baldy Mountain. There are actually 3 different peaks with separate names, but the "Baldy Bunch," as we call ourselves, refer to all 3 peaks as Baldy. People come and go on "Baldy" but the "Baldy Bunch" have been there every season for over 15 seasons. I started hunting with Bob and Danny Osmonovich on Baldy Mountain in 1983. In 1990, my son, Ole, made his first trip up Baldy. We

took a buck on the last day of the season and the "fire" was lit for him to become a hunter. Late in the afternoon, 2 years ago, Ole went back up the mountain with Danny and Bob to take his first buck in a snowstorm. He's truly one of us now!

Our camp sits in a small draw at the 4000-foot level of Baldy. To get there, you leave the paved road and travel a half hour on a gravel logging road. At the base of the mountain, the road ends at the edge of the national forest; from there, if you have a decent four-wheel-drive rig whose paint you don't care about, you can take an abandoned logging road for another 10 minutes or so. Then it's a 20-minute pack on an unmarked trail

to our camp.

The camp itself is a pole frame with plastic and nylon tarp stretched over it. It has a sheep herder's stove in it, with a couple of bent pieces of pipe coming out the top. It usually keeps us warm during the winter storm on the mountain.

What makes our camp special? Our camp is a place in our heart. It represents a brotherhood that is loyal to our sport, to our mountain and to our hunting partners. It is our friendship—it is our passion. It's where we go in October to hunt mule deer and share stories around the fire—stories of hunts on Baldy.

Camp Branstetter

Jim Jenson
Fort Collins, CO

With the start of Colorado's 1999 big game hunting season, Camp Branstetter will begin its 26th year of hunting deer and elk in the Colorado high country. After setting up camp and hunting several areas in the north central Colorado Rockies, Camp Branstetter has been located in the same campsite for the last 9 years.

Started by some of the current members' fathers and grandfathers, the camp has evolved over the years to a very comfortable and well-stocked camp. Each year we seem to add more creature comforts such as propane heat, lights and cooking equipment, ATVs, 2-way radios and, of course, cell phones. We also have found that having an electric generator for lights and to run the forced-air furnace makes for a very comfortable place to relax in the cold evenings and nights. The tent has grown through the years to the present one, which is an 18' by 52' tent with a liner and carpet for the floor. We have also added a plywood restroom with a heater and light. When hunting season closes, the only evidence of our stay is a dry, bare spot of ground surrounded by snow.

We normally have 10 or 12 members hunt the last season, which is usually about the first week of November. Camp Branstetter has been a welcome site for several lost hunters who have shown up after dark wet, cold, hungry and concerned about where they might be. After a little warmth, food and friendship, they are given a ride back to their camp to tell their hunting partners about Camp Branstetter. 🌲

The Walker Family Camp

Stephen J. Walker
Grand Rapids, MI

The Walker family white-tailed deer hunting tradition started in 1939, with my Grandpa Walker (Merrill Sr.) and some friends hunting just north of his home in Grand Rapids, Michigan. In 1940, however, the crew decided to go up to Michigan's Upper Peninsula, where Grandpa had worked in the logging camps as a youth. After interruptions for 2 wars and several more children, my Grandpa began hunting again in 1952. The next year, the camp moved a few miles to its present location outside of the village of Crystal Falls, Michigan.

The sleeping tent used for more than 40 years at the Walker Family Camp.

We stay for 10 days (8 hunting days) in a clearing that long ago was the base camp and horse stables for a logger by the name of Konia. There, we set up 2 old 14' by 16' Army style canvas tents, one for sleeping and the other for cooking and eating. We truck in all of our supplies except water, which is dipped each day from a natural spring. LP gas is used for heating and cooking. Our beds consist of sleeping bags and air mattresses set upon layers of plastic, straw and blankets.

The last year my Grandpa hunted was 1983, which was the first year I hunted. The crew now consists of his sons and grandsons (the size of the family is such that Grandpa early-on limited potential hunters to his 4

sons and their sons). My uncles, Merrill Jr. and Robert, and my dad, James, have hunted ever since they were eligible (Grandpa required that they graduate from high school first—a rule we still maintain). Along with my cousins Mark, Tom (fellow NAHC member), Tim and Mike, I am a regular each year. My brother Matt came up for the first time this year. Sadly, our crew is getting smaller, as my Uncle Robert died in October of 1997 and my dad just passed away in December of 1998.

We have been very successful over the years, getting at least 1 deer in every year except 1993 and 1997. In fact, we have harvested 134 deer in the 46 years at the present camp location (an average of just fewer than 3 per year). Grandpa got deer with the largest number of points (a 137-lb. 13-point) in 1951, while the largest deer by weight was a 221-lb. 9-point shot by Grandpa's brother-in-law in 1940. 🌲

Game Feed

Michael Brown
Winthrop Harbor, IL
Life Member

The First Baptist Church of Winthrop Harbor, Illinois, hosts a Wild Game dinner each year on the first Saturday of November. The meat is provided by the men of the church, and the ladies prepare the vegetable salads and desserts. We have 6 to 12 men go to Wyoming and Colorado to hunt deer, elk, antelope, squirrel, rabbit, pheasant and chuckars. We have bear, moose and caribou from Canada and ducks and geese as well. This year we had over 450 people from the community come for the free meal.

This is the ninth straight year for this event. We camp in tents and have a great time each year and it is great fellowship around the campfire.

Packing In: The High Sierras

John C. Damann
Lake Hughes, CA
Life Member

For the past 20 years, I have been packing into the High Sierra Mountains in Northern California. It takes about 8 months to plan a trip. The biggest and most important thing is having a good hunting party. Getting 4 or 5 guys who like to hunt and be away for a week is the first step. Next is deciding where do you want to hunt and who will pack you in. After you have that all lined up, then you need to put your camp gear together, not leaving anything out, because this is a spot camp. There are no roads or phones to have your wife bring in your deer tag that you for-

got to pack. By April or May, you should know who's going and where to go. Then it's putting all your equipment together. Most pack stations allow around 150 to 200 pounds per pack mule. Each person's gear is weighed and packed accordingly for mules.

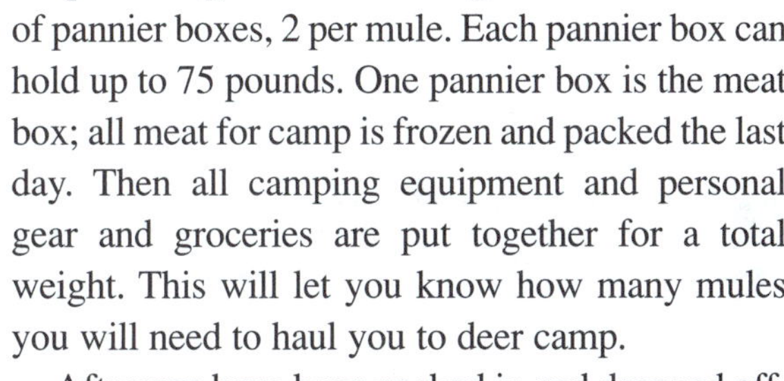

Then it's time to put the groceries together. First thing you need to do is make a menu of food for each day. Next go to the store and get all the goodies. Lastly, you have to pack the groceries and weigh it all. I have 3 sets of pannier boxes, 2 per mule. Each pannier box can hold up to 75 pounds. One pannier box is the meat box; all meat for camp is frozen and packed the last day. Then all camping equipment and personal gear and groceries are put together for a total weight. This will let you know how many mules you will need to haul you to deer camp.

After you have been packed in and dropped off, this is when everyone turns starts to put the deer

Camping Gear

- Tent, campseats
- Stove, table
- White gas
- Lanterns
- Mantels' (extra)
- Dishes, coffee pot
- Skillet, dish pans
- Rope, tape
- Tarps
- Buckets (2)
- Axes, shovel
- Can opener
- Assorted tools (hammer, pliers, saw, nails)
- Knives, forks, spoons
- Coat hangers
- Potato peeler
- Grater
- Cups
- Hot gloves
- Matches
- Fire starter

Personal Gear

- ☐ Deer rifle
- ☐ Shells
- ☐ License and deer tags
- ☐ Canteen
- ☐ Rope
- ☐ Pencil and Pen
- ☐ Insect repellent
- ☐ Hat
- ☐ Vest, jacket
- ☐ Rain gear
- ☐ Gloves
- ☐ Knife
- ☐ Camera and film
- ☐ Wipe rags
- ☐ Plastic bags
- ☐ Chapstick
- ☐ Boots
- ☐ Underwear, long johns
- ☐ Wash rag
- ☐ Bath towels
- ☐ Toothbrush and toothpaste
- ☐ Flashlight and batteries
- ☐ Sleeping bag
- ☐ Air mattress
- ☐ Blankets
- ☐ 3 warm shirts
- ☐ 6 pair socks
- ☐ Warm cap
- ☐ Camp shoes
- ☐ Rubber boots
- ☐ Pocket knife
- ☐ Deer bags

camp together. First you unload the mules, then find a good flat spot for your tent, usually under some trees in a sheltered location. Then we build the fire pit, making a rock stand to put the grill on. We then put the kitchen together using the pannier boxes for the kitchen cabinets, and we build the table for the stove and equipment. Next we all get together and get a good stack of wood for the fire. We try to get enough firewood to last the whole week and cover it with a tarp just in case it rains or snows. Keeping the wood dry is a must for cooking and warming fires. By now it's getting dark and your camp should be all together. Now it's time for dinner and just sitting around the campfire telling deer stories. The following day is opening day of your deer hunt, so everyone is in the bag by 8 p.m. On opening day it's always a challenge to bag the first and biggest buck.

The Hunt

The alarm went off at 5 a.m., the air was still and crisp, and the stars were still out with the moon fading as the sun began to rise. Jonsey was the first one up. He had already built the fire and had coffee brewing. As we lay in our warm sleeping bag, Jonsey called out, "Come on boys, the coffee is done and the bucks are jumping." By then we were up and ready. We had breakfast and put our hunting gear on. The air was still calm and chilly with the frost on the ground.

Jonsey and I would hunt together with the others hunting in the same direction. I loaded my .300 Savage, Jonsey loaded his .270 Remington, and we started across the meadows. As we approached the other side, I picked up some fresh deer tracks. I could see each hoof print in the white frost where they broke the frozen ground. There was more than one set of tracks, and they were buck tracks.

I motioned to Jonsey to come over and take a look, which he did. That is when we decided to track 'em down. I told Jonsey we would try to stay about 150 yards apart and work our way up the hill following the tracks.

Let me tell you, tracking a buck muley in the High Sierras is work. But the thrill that goes with it send chills up your back. Each step you take, you expect to see him. As I worked my way up the mountain, my steps were right on the buck's tracks. I stayed on his tracks for over an hour. The tracks went uphill, then downhill, and there were times when they went around in circles. The buck would zigzag at times and at one time I thought I had lost them. Several times I had to stop and study the tracks to figure out which way he went. But with the frost still on the ground and a little luck, I picked the buck's track up again. Each step I took, I looked ahead, trying to spot this clever buck. It was then when chills went up my back as I came across fresh buck droppings. It felt as if he were looking right at me. I continued up the mountain, taking one step at a time. Jonsey and others were out of sight but were in the same area. Within minutes it all happened. I froze in my footsteps as I was being watched by a large mule deer.

As I stood there, I raised my rifle to my shoulder. My knees were starting to shake as I focused the scope on the deer. It was a buck, and as I squeezed the trigger, he started running. At that same moment, another large muley jumped up. I began to run up the hill, trying to locate the spot where I had shot my buck. When I approached the spot, I could not see any deer or blood. For a moment I thought I had missed him. I thought to myself that I had to have hit him because it was only 100 yards at the most. As I started to backtrack my steps attempting to locate the buck's tracks, I spotted him. I had bagged my buck on opening day! When I got to him I observed that he had a good rack of antlers. He was a four and three. I jumped with joy before settling down to field-dress my buck.

But the hunt was not over. As I was cleaning and tying up my buck for the drag back to camp, I heard the crack of Jonsey's .270 going off. I then heard Jonsey cry out. "Hey John! Over here! Hey John!" As I looked over to the location of Jonsey, I could see that he had shot the other big buck. I left my buck and ran over to see his buck; Jonsey had also bagged a nice 4-point muley. Then we both jumped with joy. I helped him clean and prepare the buck for the drag back to camp. By this time the rest of the hunting party had arrived and helped us with the dragging.

When we arrived at camp, we hung the bucks on a deer pole in the trees to give them a good cleaning. Then we wrapped them in a deer bag. What a day it was! Over the past 20 years we have taken some very nice mule deer home with us. And there were some years when we were all skunked. But it's the kind of deer trip you never forget when you live for a week in the High Sierras at 10,000 feet.

Unita Mountains Camp

Brian Hastings
Green River, UT
Life Member

This is my hunting camp in the Unita Mountains in northeastern Utah. As you can see it was a little chilly that season. Our camp was set up not too far from Rasmussen Lake at approximately 13,000 feet.

We built the lean-to to keep the weather blocked off and to keep ourselves and our firewood dry. This was one of the best hunting trips that my buddy, Brad Ryan, and I have probably ever been on, even though we were both empty-handed when we went home. In that week-long trip we developed a bond and memories to last a lifetime.

The "Golden Rule" Deer Hunting Camp

Erik Derleth
Berlin, WI

The "Golden Rule" Deer Hunting Camp was established in 1923 in northern Wisconsin. The camp has been a tent camp since 1923 and continues to be a tent camp. With no electricity, no telephones, no indoor plumbing, it's life without modern conveniences for 9 days. What a way to go!

The camp was started by Frank Kraut Sr., Frank Jr. and other hunting partners from Curtis, Wisconsin. Frank Kraut Jr. was 14 years old when the camp started. He has hunted every year since 1923, including this past season, where he celebrated his 89th birthday on November 18th, in camp. Referred to as "the fox" because of his quiet and patient hunting skills, Frank has shot more than 70 whitetail bucks and has a story to go along with each one.

Hank Derleth Sr., from Beaver Dam, Wisconsin, joined the camp in 1933. Frank Kraut Jr. and he became close friends as teammates on the Chippewa Marines semi-pro football team. The Marines played the Green Bay Packers and Chicago Bears in those days. They had many memorable seasons together and enjoyed a lifetime friendship.

Hank Derleth Jr. joined the camp in 1949 and has since become the full-time camp cook. Three of his sons, Peter, Erik and Mike, along with

Frank's nephew, Dick Bentley, make up the current camp.

Thursday before opening day, which is a Saturday in Wisconsin, is "moving-in day." The camp is located 300 yards from the nearest logging road, where we park our trucks. All equipment—tents, stoves, heaters, food, beverages, guns, clothes and bedding—is carried to the camp area via toboggans and hands. Over the years we have found that toboggans work the best for moving in. They work excellent when there is snow, but require a little mule power when there is no snow (a great way to get in shape for the coming deer drives).

Current hunters/outdoorsmen are surprised when they hear we hunt out of a tent, concerned that it might be too cold, but as our old-timers in camp are fond of saying, "We haven't froze an egg yet." The actual tent size is 14' x 16' x 10' high in the center with 4' side walls. The front end consists of the cooking/eating area with the back end being the sleeping quarters. It takes all day to pitch the tent, and set up the bunk, set up the wood burning stove, table and cook area.

One camp tradition consists of having a shot of brandy when "smoke comes out of the chimney" for the first time. This requires that the tent, wood burn-

ing stove, and stove pipes be set up. When smoke comes out of the chimney for the first time, we know we'll be warm and dry for the next 9 days, so a brandy bottle is passed in celebration. (What to do if your fire goes out? Start another fire and have another shot!)

Over the years, some humorous things have occurred around the fire-starting event. Frank Jr. is in charge of checking the stove pipes to make sure "all is clear"; knowing this, one year, Hank Sr. lit some paper and cardboard just before Frank went to check. Needless to say, as Frank looked over the edge of the stove pipe, the first bellows of black smoke came belching forth. Frank got a face full of soot and came out looking like Al Jolson.

But the most profound tradition is the coming together of family: grandfathers, sons, grandsons, uncles and nephews. Since 1923, we have hunted and camped in the same area, never tiring of the setting up and breaking down of the camp, the scenery, or the fact that there is no electricity or indoor plumbing. For us it is a welcome break from everyday life. 🌲

Prairie Deer Camp

Kal Sears
North Platte, NE

From the deserts of Arizona, the swamps of Florida, and the cold forests of Canada, I have spent over 40 years in deer camps. From a 38' motor home to sleeping under a canvas, I've done them all. Some have been more comfortable, some more conventional and others, scenic. I've enjoyed them all and would love to step back in time to each of them. From the Coues, along the Mexican border, mulies of Montana, or trophy whitetails in a dozen or so other states, I've loved them all. I've never met a deer camp I didn't like. From our friend in Alaska and his "1001 Campfires," I have also had the same pleasures and may they go on forever. The evenings are not charged against one's allotted time on earth.

So it is that I reach back to one such camp north of Douglas, Wyoming. On the treeless prairies where the only sounds at twilight are the wind, the mournful calls of the coyotes and the crackling of a campfire.

My brother Don and I bowhunted mule deer for 7 days without a chance for a shot and never once complained. I like to believe that we hunt for all the right reasons. We came back to this same area for 3 years and even took a couple nice bucks, but in the chapters of life, to both of us this was "A Deer Camp."

Boys to Men

Daniel A. Garmon
Ventura, CA

Our hunting camp started out as a 16' x 20' tent. After a few years of use I decided we needed a little more room, so I had what we call a porch made, and now the tent is 16' x 34'. We use the front to cook and as a general storage area and the back as a dining hall and sleeping quarters.

One of the traditions in our camp is at the end of each hunt, I use a black marker and write on the inside roof of the tent the year, where we are hunting and who killed what. It's kind of like a history book in the making of our camp. I have sat in camp with friends after a long day hunting and relived hunts of yesteryear many nights reading what we call "hunter hieroglyphics" on the roof of the tent. I will pass this tent on down to my nephews and they will have some history to share with the young hunters they take to deer camp.

I have shared this camp with many good hunters; the regulars are my nephew Danny Garmon, my long time hunting partner and best friend

Dennis Morgan, his son Joe Morgan, Kent Wheeler and many others.

I have set camp in most all of the Western states. We have hunted blacktail, mulies and whitetail out of this camp along with most all big game the west has to offer. I have seen young boys come in to deer camp and go home young men.

A Deer Camp in Boston! (New York)

Gary Shore
Kenmore, NY

I am an avid deer hunter with an 80-acre camp located in beautiful Boston, New York, approximately 35 miles south of Buffalo.

My camp can best be described as spartan. I hunt out of an old truck camper with propane heat and light. On a good night, I can get the camper up to 50 degrees at best; it beats the back of a pickup!

We have some fantastic deer hunting here in western New York and I love my camp!

My wife and I plan to build a cabin soon. As much as I'm looking forward to that, I know I'll always cherish all my memories of my "spartan camp."

Heck, who needs all the comforts of home? When you're hunting whitetails, that's all you need!

Mel's Deer Hunting Shack

Melvin Hladky
Minnetonka, MN

My deer hunting camp is a 1956 Ford bus. We have hunted in the same area for the past 41 years—just north of Aiken, Minnesota.

This old bus has gone up to camp for 21 years. For the last 10 years, I have owned the bus myself. It has an electric refrigerator, a gas stove and oven, a forced air LP gas furnace and a 60-amp service entrance. The bus sleeps 4 people very comfortably.

At one time I had a 110-volt gas generator on the back of the bus, but now I plug into a meter pole at my friend's property where we hunt.

Last year I got a nice 8-point buck! 🌲

The Warmest Place I Know

Tom Kleist
Eagle Lake, MN

A thin layer of clear plastic, now becoming opaque with duct tape patching, is supported by a 2 x 2 framework of borrowed building materials; the shack is the warmest place I know.

Heat, and an orange glow, is cast by a rust-thin barrel stove. The strong, hazy scent of wood smoke is overpowered, however, by the dank smell of split pine, wet wool and two-bit cigars. Heat, as a by-product of light produced by two gas lanterns, is released with a continuous, solemn hiss.

Twelve warm bodies, some calling this place home and others visiting, cram into the one-room shack that is now insulated with blaze Gore-Tex, polar fleece and wool hung from undersized hooks. Experiences are exchanged, stories are told, and there is laughter. Young ears listen, trying to hear 4 different speakers. I listen too and wait patiently to hear familiar stories, those told annually, to see how much has changed from the last time the story was told. Here is one: I have heard it for 16 seasons and

know it word for word but still sit transfixed. We both conclude—me silently, he out loud with a melodious laugh, "I've shot a few deer in my day."

As supper draws near (breakfast at 5 a.m., lunch in a tree at noon, and supper is only near at 7:30 p.m.), I walk our company to the door. Outside, my nose welcomes the cold, clean air. A zillion tiny stars and a solitary silver moon light the sky, and snow mirrors it back to my eye. As I laugh and say goodbye, my breath drifts towards the yard light, and I follow it to the shack. An old red lantern, lashed to a sapling tripod, throws a dingy yellow light that is surprisingly welcome. Returning from each day's hunt, night chasing me home, the yard light beckons, signaling home.

Amid laughter from the inside, I pause at the thermometer attached to the "Kleist Hilton" sign. Someone is always laughing in deer camp. I note the temperature (9°F) and straighten the Hilton sign. The cold hurries me back in; as the door slams behind me, I remove fogged lenses and smile. Deer camp is the companionship; I am glad I am here. I join the laughter and am warm spiritually too.

Idaho Wilderness Camp

Lanny Olson
Puyallup, WA

Our hunting camp in Idaho isn't just about deer, or deer hunting, for that matter. It's about people. Good people who come together once a year for an adventure. It's about food, good food to be shared with old friends and new friends we make every year. It's about some of the most beautiful environment we know. And yes, there are deer—some big ones. There are elk and Rocky Mountain sheep. There are native cutthroat in the river. And there is sunshine, rain, snow and wind. And there is the warmth and safety of the camp where we all share all of this.

Let me tell you about it.

My hunting partner, Rich Devine, and I begin our trip in the Seattle area where we put together the provisions required to make a comfortable month-long camp deep in the Idaho wilderness. Over the years we have learned that if we can squeeze it into Rich's pickup, we can get into the remote camp in

two airplanes. So once the provisions have been loaded, we leave the Seattle area at 2 a.m. and drive to the small airport in central Idaho where the provisions are packed into the small airplanes for the 45-minute flight into the camp location.

When we get there, there most likely will not be anyone else there. Nor will there be any radio, television, roads, cars or cell phones. But as weeks pass, other camps do start to arrive, but generally not until at least two weeks have past. So this is the time for relaxing, watching deer and elk and maybe a Rocky Mountain sheep. It is time for fishing in the river for the native trout. It is time for eating. It is time for storytelling and sometimes the same stories as last year, but the deer and fish somehow get bigger, but that is okay, because we are older now too.

The country is tough. It is some of the most remote and rugged country in the lower U.S. Everything we use, wear, or eat must be flown in. The game we pursue must be found by hiking up and down some of the difficult country you can imagine. So, we must be prepared both physically and logistically. I think, though, over the years, we are more prepared logistically than physically, although for us having as many hunting years under our belts as we do, we get around pretty good.

Our base home in the mountains is a 12' x 14' tent set up not far from the small airplane runway where all of our goods have been flown. This home is as comfortable as any home we could have anywhere. It is warm and dry in the worst of weather and wind. We have developed over the years an arrangement that serves as both packing boxes and a kitchen. We have the tent with a kerosene heater that keeps the tent warm and doubles as a cook stove. One of the rules of camp is that the first one up in the morning turns the heater on and sets the coffee on top. After about 20 minutes, the tent is warm and the smell of perking coffee saturates the tent. Not a bad way to wake up—providing you are not the first one up. (Note: The trick is to feed your hunting partner one or more cups of coffee before he goes to bed. Guarantee you will be able to hold it longer than he will in the morning.)

We bring the best food into camp. With some preparation, food will last the full month because the weather cools down to the lower twenties at night and acts just like a refrigerator/freezer. So, with some creativity, we create exceptionally good meals not expected in this remote area. And it is the food that has been the catalyst that has brought together many wonderful people who are the focus of many memorable experiences.

There was the pineapple upside-down cake made in my dutch oven that made a lifelong friend out of Bob Dana, a pilot out of Stanley, Idaho. There was the stack of pancakes and bacon served to Cameron Hershaw and his hunting partner from Palouse, Washington, who had run a little short of supplies. Cam says the meal saved his life. (Well, I really don't think it did; it only felt like it did, Cam.) There was the birthday cake baked for George and Heather Coats's daughter who could not join her parents in hunting camp. (We really did enjoy her birthday cake, though.) There were the Alaskan clams Jim Pieschel and Marion Gray cooked for Rich and me the first year we shared a camp. There were fresh Alaskan salmon we ate with Curt Rudy and his son Andy from Elma, Washington.

And there were the experiences we shared. There was the day the tent became the "mash unit" when Dr. Leo Mack from Tyler, Texas, and I sewed up a badly cut hand using a sewing needle and pliers. When the hunter got to town a few days later, the hospital said there wasn't anything they needed to do. Good job, Dr. Lee. There was the time a horse bucked me into the frozen

river with a deer on my back. The water was cold and deep, and the walk back to camp was no picnic, but all turned out well. There was the day that Rich and I saw elk, deer, and Rocky Mountain sheep in the same canyon at the same time. There was the first hunt for my son Lee, who was finally able to take time out from his job with the Seattle Mariners to finally experience for himself how rugged these "hills" really were. Your old man did you in, right Lee?

There were the people too. Over the 15 years or so that I have been going to this place, I have met many wonderful people. In fact, I cannot recall one person who was not a very enjoyable person. No one I know has lost a single thing to theft. In fact, every year when people leave, they leave their excess goods for those who remain. One year, Jerry (a hunter from Olympia, Washington) spent a night in our tent while we were in bivouc camp and left $5 on the table.

Once in a while, a new group of hunters will hear about our location and fly in to see what the hunting is like. Usually not knowing how best to pack for this type of hunt, they are often conservative and bring along minimal provisions. So Rich and I take delight in preparing fried chicken, mashed potatoes and gravy for dinner. The trick is to prepare way more than we can eat, then open the tent door awhile. There is nothing, and I mean nothing, that smells as good as frying chicken in a really remote wilderness. Just before it is ready, and after a few minutes of fine chicken aroma, one of us will go over to the new group and ask if they would like to come over for dinner. Instant new friends.

Yes, there are the deer. Both Rich and I can remember every deer we have taken. We can remember the deer we have packed out of deep canyons and carried down steep mountains. We can remember the deer we have not taken just as well. We can remember where and when we saw them. Maybe we will see them if some other hunter takes them, and that is just fine, because most likely we will relive their hunt over dinner or a beer and it is just as satisfying.

Our hunting camp is people, and it is food. It is preparation for a whole year ahead of time. It is experiences and pristine environment. It is stories and laughter. It is exhaustion and exhilaration. It is sounds and smells. It is friendship of the best kind.

But mostly it is memories.

Ruby Mountains, Nevada

Wayne Culberson
San Jose, CA

I look forward to the hunting season every year. My hunting partners and I apply for the late-season deer hunts in the state of Nevada every year. We all are California residents and enjoy the great outdoors.

During a cold fall, to be successful in the hunt it is very important to be able to sleep warm and keep dry after a long day of hunting. So remember to keep the firewood stacked up and keep the stove burning.

Blue Goose

Jerome J. Bolle
Manitowoc, WI

We have been hunting white-tailed deer with the "blue goose" in northeastern Wisconsin for the past 19 years. Three of the four hunters who use the bus also worked to convert it to a hunting cabin. We drive the bus into the Black Sam Swamp, onto a dead-end trail, park it and hunt the entire 9-day Wisconsin season.

We only have a couple of traditions—our steak and baked potato (over the grill), Thanksgiving dinner and watching the Green Bay Packers win and Dallas lose. We bring up all of our supplies, leaving the woods maybe once to restock the beer, I mean food.

During hunting season we live by the motto: The woods is our home and the wind is our comb. ♣

Okanogan County Camp

William Cooper
Bothell, WA
Life Member

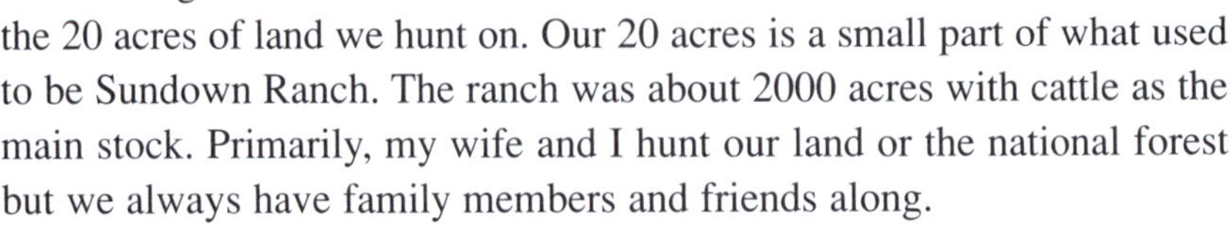

Our deer camp is located in the northeast part of Washington state. We hunt mule and black-tailed deer. Our camp is in Okanogan County, 1 mile north of the Okanogan National Forest. We own the 20 acres of land we hunt on. Our 20 acres is a small part of what used to be Sundown Ranch. The ranch was about 2000 acres with cattle as the main stock. Primarily, my wife and I hunt our land or the national forest but we always have family members and friends along.

We drive 6 hours from our home to get to heaven-on-earth; we get there about 4 to 6 times per year. We always take plenty of chipmunk food with us. As soon as we park our motor home, the chipmunks run to their feeding rock. We put the food on the rock and then watch them play and eat from inside the RV.

Allegheny Mountain Camp

Mike Perkins
Franklinton, NC

Over the years, longtime hunting buddies from Virginia and North Carolina gather in the Allegheny Mountains for one week of camaraderie, cold nights, bad food and storytelling!

Camp is set up about 2 miles from the nearest road. All gear is packed in and packed out. A lot of people say that we are crazy to go to such great lengths on setting up this camp, but the quality of the hunt is worth it!

The yearly members of the camp are: Jim Warren—retired Navy Chief and farmer; Lonnie, his son—a coastal environmental engineer; James, Lonnie's son; Ed Haverlack—USFS wildlife biologist; and Mike Perkins—construction manager.

It's hard work setting up camp each year but we all know that the true pleasure is being with nature in a beautiful mountain setting with good friends. We share the experiences that we gather this one week with many people throughout the year.

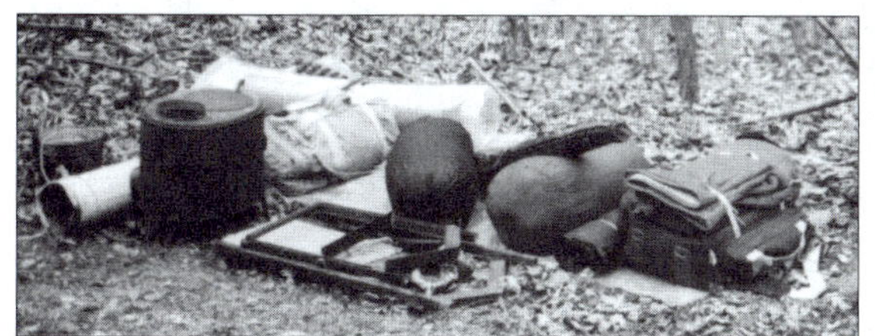

Oh, by the way, we usually are quite successful in harvesting a buck!

Story of the "Track Stew Outing"

David Koplar & Gerald Maher
Torrington, CT
Life Members

Yeah! "Track Stew Outing"—that's what we call this week-long trip as we stacked a couple of logs on the fire. It was a cold and snowy December night in a Connecticut swamp, and we huddled closer to the fire for warmth. We discovered the recipe for Track Stew that evening. Just gather up a pound of fresh, clean deer tracks, toss them into a pot, pour in a can of Dinty Moore, mix gently, heat and eat. Delicious! We ate a lot of Track Stew that year and the name caught on. The Track Stew Outing was born! Little did we realize at the time that the Track Stew Outing would become an annual event for the next 18 years.

Gerry and I were fledgling deer hunters out on our first big game hunting adventure. We both longed to hunt at some exotic locale, but our budgets fell short of our dreams. So with a little luck, lots of imagination and permits for private land, our dreams came true. It wasn't Montana or Canada, but a forest can play tricks on your mind, if you let it. Traffic noise was wind blow-

ing through the coulees. Far-off lights became new constellations, and barking dogs were wolves signaling the pack. The game warden, who checked our permits, thought we were a little strange to be out camping in this weather. To tell you the truth, we began to question our sanity as well.

The first few years we hauled all our equipment and stuff atop an old toboggan. As you can imagine, the camp was a pretty spartan affair. Gradually over the years, our accommodations improved. The 2-person tent was replaced with a spacious plastic-sheet lean-to. Its large jutting roof and side wings created a cavern-like structure that captured the fire's heat and, compliments of a fickle wind, the smoke. Then, 15 years ago, we received permits to hunt a chunk of heaven on private land in Litchfield. We began scouting out this paradise for deer, and a campsite, while mapping out landmarks and hunting strategies. We found an animal skeleton in Bone Valley. You could set your watch by the deer in 4:30 Valley. Acorn Slopes and Blueberry Ridge were the feeding areas. Years later, we received permits to hunt the Great Beyond, an adjacent property. Soon places nicknamed Death Valley, Hemlock Grove, Wolf Tree Ridge, and Over the Edge, were added to our mental maps. We've taken a lot of deer while on the Track Stew Outings.

Over the years, we've had many memorable experiences while on the Track Stew Outing. One year we had permits to hunt the foothills of Dudleytown, a legendary haunted ghost town in northwest Connecticut. It might have been a combination of mischievous spirits and campfire stories that spooked us each night, but we never returned to that place again. While still-hunting through the nasties on a drizzly misty day, I spotted a sunbeam shining down on one tree in Bone Valley. Figuring it was a good omen, I climbed the tree, sat on a branch and shot my very first deer 10 minutes later. That tree over the years has yielded an abundance of mighty fine deer.

During another trip, the state was hammered by a fearsome blizzard. The roads were closed, power lines were down and the temperature plummeted. Our friends, fearing we may have perished, mounted a daring rescue, only to find us cozy and snug in camp, sitting next to a crackling fire, snacking on venison teriyaki, while sipping a liberal libation.

Rituals and omens seem to play an important role in our hunting camp. We found the headboard of a crib with cutesy pictures of a bambi in bells smiling at two bear cubs in bows, climbing a tree for a camp mascot. Go ahead, laugh, but on that trip, I shot a 4-pointer in the morning and Gerry took a spike in the afternoon from the same treestand.

A blazing fire is central to our camp. For years, we gathered wood from blowdowns to feed it, but now we have a cord of wood delivered. The fire not only gives us warmth and light, but I cook our special treats on it as well. Venison roasted over a hardwood fire and sweet potatoes baked in the coals are a meal fit for royalty. Gerry likes big roaring campfires. One year the temperature hovered around minus five degrees outside, but in the lean-to, it was a balmy 40 degrees.

After 18 years, we have grown in wisdom, technique and toys. Both of us now drive 4 x 4's, so the camp is much more luxurious than it once was. (I will admit that one year we did suffer a bit. I forgot the brown sugar and cinnamon for our baked apples.) Our accommodations have evolved, too. The lean-to has been replaced by a pop-up tent camper. The cavernous jutting roof and sides are still added for comfort. Gerry's 4 x 4 quad is a real big help for dragging deer into camp these days. This year for the first time ever, we had "Monday Night Football," run by a power converter, hooked up to a truck battery. Cellular phones were also added, for safety reasons. I wonder if Pizza Hut delivers out there? Every Wednesday night since the beginning, out friends gather around the welcoming campfire. They come out to celebrate life and swap tales of adventure gone by and yet to come. Life is good and only getting better.

That once-in-a lifetime hunting trip can be yours with a little luck, imagination, proper permits and a hunting buddy that's easily misled. You don't need a ton of money for an exotic adventure. We have one every year in "Montana," Connecticut. Dreams can come true. It can happen to you, if you're young at heart, and being a little crazy helps, too. Hopefully the Track Stew Outings will live on forever.

Life, Liberty and the Pursuit of Happiness ... and White-Tailed Deer! 🌲

Traditions in the Huron National Forest

Mart Van Stee
Kentwood, MI

I am Mart Van Stee, 78 years of age, an avid hunter and outdoorsman. My camp is in the Huron National Forest, on government land in Alcona County, Michigan.

We just concluded my 51st continuous camp, interrupted only by 2 years of service in the Pacific Theater in WWII. Our crew consists of my son, Marshall, his 2 sons, Jay and Chris, my son-in-law, Bob, his son, Rob and myself. This year, 2 friends also came along as our guests.

We employ no guides, relying solely on our memories and compass readings. We allow no alcohol during the hunt.

Our camp is (and always has been) a "tent" camp, where each member helps with the chores: wood cutting, cooking, trash removal, etc. Our main tent is large, 16' x 24', with a conventional wooden door and a barrel stove that keeps us comfortable. We do our cooking on a 4-burner propane stove in a smaller tent (8' x 12'). Snowfall on our second day caused the smaller tent's ridgepole to break one year and it was promptly repaired using the trunk of a young 2" poplar tree—so plentiful in this forest.

The terrain is not particularly hilly, but swampland teaches us utmost caution. One year, one of our men found himself in frigid, waist deep water after stepping on a patch of spongy soil! Fortunately, 2 of our boys were close by! After getting him on dry land, they each removed some of their outerwear and, once he got out of his wet clothes, they got him dressed and back to camp—cold but safe.

After the day's hunt, we have our main meal and build a large campfire out of burned-out pine stumps, where good-natured bragging and lying are the order of the day. Well after dark, when the weather is just right, the Northern Lights are fabulous—presenting a dazzling, unforgettable display of color and motion. In the stillness of the winter's night, creatures of the forest present a cacophony of screeches, howls, screams—all music to a woodsman's ears.

After breaking camp, we take all our trash to a dumpster in a small town, approximately 15 miles from camp, leaving the area in better condition than when we arrived.

As the photo shows, we are almost always successful. This year we took a 9-point, a 4-point and a spike. Our ongoing success rate is approximately 60 percent. 🌲

The Good Times Are Now

Ed Janik
Lemont, IL

We go each November to the national forest in northern Wisconsin. We all see old photos in bars or in magazines from the 1930s, '40s, '50s, and yes, even '60s. Some of us wish were there right now ... well this is as close as we've gotten.

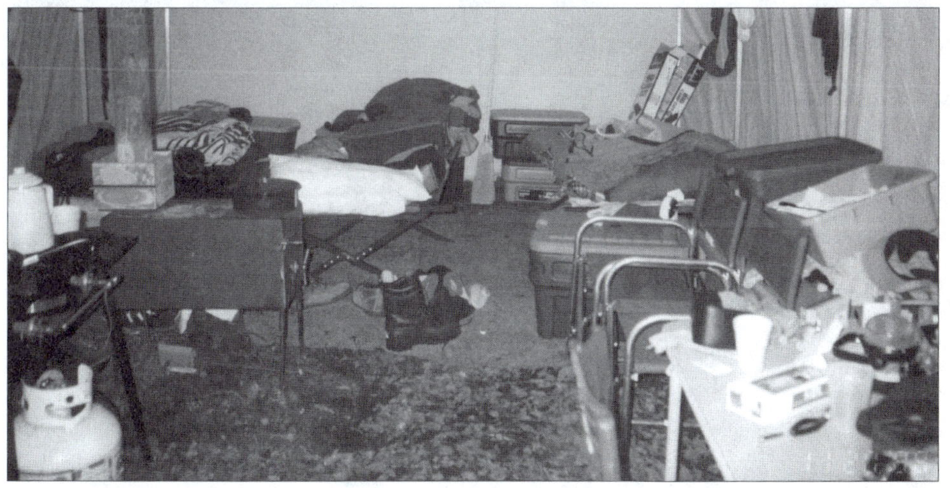

The Lieutenant's Quarters

Daryl E. Davis
Walton, KY
Life Member

Here is our deer camp in Wheatly, Kentucky, where we're totally self-sufficient for all 10 days of the season.

Life Members Stan Meadows, Randy Meadows, David Byrd and I have enjoyed this outing for more than 10 years with much success.

The lodge is modeled after a pre-1840 Lieutenant Colonel's quarters, which we use for primitive rendezvous throughout the year.

Gogebic County Deer Camp

John Kimball
Ironwood, MI

Our camp is portable—a 14' x 24' tent. Each year since 1979 we have assembled our skeleton frame and put up our tent on public land here in Gogebic County in the Upper Peninsula of Michigan. The area we hunt is very remote. We must truck in our gear by 4-wheel drive. We are 3 1/2 miles from the nearest forest service road.

The tent is very warm, comfortable and roomy. When we put it up, we start with a layer of vissquern on the floor. Then we put carpeting, yes, carpeting, wall to wall. We have shelves, 3 sets of bunks, a couch, chairs, picnic table, propane cook stove and lights, and a 55-gallon barrel stove that uses wood.

I hunt here along with my son, my dad, my brother, and my brother-in-law. I am 42 years old and have hunted since I was 14. I have been coming to this spot for 27 seasons now. In fact, I have sat at the same spot for 27 seasons and have taken 32 bucks there. My largest buck was an 8-point scoring 137, and my dad has gotten a 10-point scoring 146. Not much to brag about, but pretty good for up here.

The fun we have and the memories made are priceless. By looking at this tent from the outside, people ask how we can stay in such a thing. Well, it's quite enjoyable. It's dry, warm and fun!

Putting up and maintaining this kind of camp is a lot of work but it's worth every minute of it. Also, if you think the last day of hunting season is sad, that's nothing compared to how we feel when it's time to break camp and go home until next year.

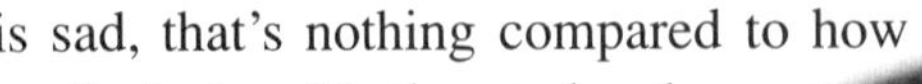

A G.P. Medium

Gary Coffey
Bob Page
Crete, NE

Our deer camp is located in the Nebraska National Forest, which is about 230 miles from our home in Crete, Nebraska. We started to organize camp in 1985. As we had no motel reservations, our first camp was a pickup with a camper shell. From there we tried campers, but never felt like that was the answer.

The 2 of us who had started hunting together met a man from Lincoln, Nebraska, who made his own wall tents. We purchased a 13' x 17' wall tent with no ridgepoles or stakes for $150. After a few attempts, we came up with a ridgepole that collapses and folds into itself for easy transport. Sand stakes were made from rebar and plate steel. This tent was a great asset to our camp, but we soon realized it would not be large enough for the number of people we envisioned using our camp. As we were still using campers to sleep in, we still didn't think we had the camaraderie that we were after. We needed a bigger tent!

With plans to use our wall tent for a mess tent, our search began for a tent large enough for us to sleep in. Through a co-worker, we learned that his brother-in-law had purchased some large tents from a military base several years earlier. Upon contacting this person we discovered he still had the tents and would be will-

ing to sell us one. A military tent was delivered to my house shortly thereafter. It turned out to be a 16' x 16' officer tent that was full of dry rot. We called back and were told that he had a couple others we could look at. Off we were on a 300-mile road trip in hopes of finding the tent of our dreams!

Luckily, the next one was in a lot better shape, but it wasn't the same size. It turned out to be 16' x 32'—a G.P. medium, in military terms. We paid him $50 for another tent with no ridgepoles or stakes and no idea how to put it up. With luck, another friend had a similar-sized tent, so we were able to get measurements and instructions and in no time had it standing. Now we had the perfect camp, or so we thought. By this time our camp had grown from just a few of us to as many as 18 people.

The mess tent worked great for feeding all of us, but there wasn't enough room for cooking ... enter my father-in-law! Owning an upholstery shop, he helped us add on to the mess tent. With an 8' x 13' addition to the front of the tent, we now had a 13' x 25' mess tent large enough to cook and eat in.

Our next purchase turned out to be a store-bought ice fishing shack that we use for our outhouse. As we have to haul everything from firewood to toilet paper into and out of the forest, it's a necessity for everything to collapse or fold up.

Deer camp has always been family oriented, our youngest starting at age 8 and our oldest (my father) at age 74. We have had 10 father-son combinations, and at least that many brother combinations. Our other brotherhood connection is that with our local fire department, as most of us have or are serving our community. This connection is also the one requirement needed to get invited into camp!

Our success rate is not as outstanding as other parts of the state, but we have always brought venison home, which we butcher ourselves. Success to us is not in how many deer we bring home, but in being with best friends and family in one of the most beautiful places in the state!   🌲

Selkirk Mountain Camp

Tom Thompson
Spokane, WA

Our camp is located in the Selkirk Mountain Range in northeast Washington. Fellow NAHC member Mike Moore and I have had our camp there for 8 years now. We hunt whitetail, mule deer, elk, bear and cougar from our camp. Our camp consists of a 16' x 16' army tent with a 30' x 50' poly tarp as a rainfly. I do the cooking and Mike does the dishes. I am making a new stove for next season; it will have an oven and a hot water tank on it. We are getting this camp so nice that it is just like being at home.

It doesn't really matter if we take any game or not; we just enjoy being outdoors. We always hate for the season to be over and can't wait for it to start again so we can get back to our camp.

We try to do as much scouting in the summer as we can. We don't see very many people during the season, because it's a pretty rough area to hunt, but we like it that way.

CHAPTER three

<u>Building A Dream</u>

We often learn to build before we learn to walk. As kids, many of us enjoyed the challenge of building with everything from Lincoln Logs to Legos, bringing farmhouses, bridges, dump trucks and an infinite number of other interesting objects to life. As adults, many of us never lose that passion to build. The camps included in this chapter offer evidence that some kids never grow up. And dreams—especially dreams of bringing a one-of-a-kind deer camp to life—never die.

Foxfire Cabin

Connie Jenkins
John Day, OR

My husband and his father built the 2-story, 2-room cabin in 1975. Plans were designed from the "Foxfire book" series. It's approximately 20' x 20' and all the materials to build it came from the property it sits on, or through bartering with friends. Even the wood stove that heats it was a freebie won in a poker game!

The cabin sits on 160 acres of leased ground surrounded by 5000 acres of state land in the beautiful countryside of Cyler, New York. It offers prime shotgun and archery hunting for white-tailed deer, turkey and grouse.

Although we live on the West Coast, every chance we get, we go back to the cabin to chase out the raccoons, enjoy the sights and do some hunting.

In a few more years, we'll start taking our son on these hunting trips and continue the tradition of hunting out of the cabin in New York.

The Ultimate Hunting Camp

Boats West
Pineville, LA

Several years back when my wife and I first moved to central Louisiana, my greatest concern was "where would I hunt?" Miss Pam, on the other hand, was concerned about finding a house and a church and getting acquainted with the community. As luck would have it I was introduced to Mike DeKeyzer. Out of that initial meeting grew a friendship and the opportunity to join a group that he hunted with up in Winn Parish.

Of the members in the club, there were four of us who struck up a special relationship: Mike, Paul Stitch, Jay Isacks and me. Our enthusiasm for hunting ranged from casual to fanatical (with Jay and me falling into the latter category). All of us have reached that point in life where the creature comforts and good food are as critical to us as the number and quality of the resident deer herd on the lease.

For me, these three guys were the ideal huntin' buddies. Mike and Jay are both architects, and Paul is the General Manager of a steel fabricating plant.

Since my "mechanical aptitude" is slightly lower than that of a stone, it was really handy having someone in camp who could actually fix stuff. All three of these fellas are also excellent cooks. Given that my culinary skills are even *less* than my mechanical skills, this was critical to the survival of our relationship. When I joined the club, these guys had been camping out in a pop-up camper the previous couple years. One day we put our heads together and decided that what we needed were more permanent and, or course, comfortable accommodations. I believe this decision came right after six of us spent the night in the pop-up camper in a torrential downpour following a meal of Cajun red beans, sausage and rice.

What evolved amazes me. We got together with the Cox brothers, David and Herbert, who are members of our club and live on the edge of our lease, to see if we could put our camp house on their property. Their mom agreed to lease us a piece of ground. It was decided that we would purchase a portable building rather than attempting to construct the camp house from the ground up (especially since deer season was about to open). The first season in the camp house was about what I would have imagined for a hunting camp. Our 12' x 24' steel building was in place. It was not insulated and we had no running water or electricity. The only luxury we had was a porta-john that Paul had brought up to the camp.

Until then, I had done all of my hunting up north and it was difficult for me to accept that it would get cold down here in Louisiana. I still shiver when I remember that first night when the temperature dropped below freezing and I was lying there in my bunk with just a single blanket over me. That uninsulated steel building was like an icebox. After putting on every piece of clothing that I had with me, plus piling on any loose piece of clothing in the building, I vowed to get myself the warmest sleeping bag I could buy. The next morning (or afternoon) when we had thawed out and our teeth stopped chattering enough for us to speak, we began planning for improvements to our camp house.

Once that deer season ended, we set about implementing our improvements. The weekends we spent working on the camp house were enough to make Bob Villa cringe and Tim the Tool Man smile. I now know the importance of the expression "measure once, cut twice" (or is it the other way around?). First we had the building wired for electricity. That summer we also added a 12' x 24' covered porch. We insulated the walls, put up paneling and laid down vinyl floor covering. Since it was in the middle of summer when we did all this work, we also felt the need to install an air conditioner and a ceiling fan. There are two electric space heaters, but with my new cold-weather sleeping bag it tends to get too warm to sleep comfortably when they are both turned on.

As nice as this may sound, we were still "roughing it." Although we had a refrigerator, we did not have running water and had to cook our meals on a Coleman stove or the propane grill. By our third season, we had finally begun to get life a bit more tolerable. Now we have running water, an electric cookstove, electric coffee maker and a microwave. The kitchen cabinets and counter top with double stainless steel sinks are nicer than what's in my house. The only concessions we have made to "roughing it" are that we do not have hot water (yet!) and we still have to trek out to the porta-john to answer the call of nature. Mike does have plans for adding a full bathroom at one end of our porch. Did I mention that we also have a TV and VCR (but no cable)?

One of the things I have noticed this year ... Miss Pam no longer threatens to make me go and stay at the hunting camp when I have been especially forgetful or insensitive. Now when I load up to go to the camp she asks, "you are coming home, aren't you?"

Although we are not quite there, we are continuing to strive to create the ultimate deer camp. There is an inherent danger to having your camp house too comfortable. On those cold, rainy and downright nasty mornings it is difficult to motivate yourself to go out into the woods. 🌲

Sawyer Brook Camp

Rusty Parker
Lynn, MA

I purchased the land in 1987 and built my cabin in December of 1988. The camp is located in North Andover, which is in the deep western mountains of Maine, overlooking Sawyer Brook. The terrain is rocky and steep, and the deer are few, approximately 4 to 6 per square mile, but after years of hunting the area and learning their travel routes, success rates have been good. I've taken 3 bucks over 200 pounds. And my father and brother have also filled their tags.

We meet the third week of November each year with much anticipation. We spend time hunting, riding ATVs and visiting other camps, where stories abound. The Wednesday of deer week we go to a ho-down where we eat and drink and listen to great music and where "he who misses—does the dishes!"

One camp owner in the area, Roger Conant, sends a newsletter out each year and has given us Indian names; my name is Ridge Runner. He tells of tales past and present. I look forward to these letters each year.

Spending deer season with family and friends at my cabin is beyond words, but I am happy to share it here with you. 🌲

Susquahahna County Deer Camp

Charlie Sears
Kingston, MA

I am proud to tell you about our hunting camp, which is located on 75 acres of prime deer country in Susquahahna County, Pennsylvania. When I was a young boy, I would read about those who went to camps to hunt. Little did I know that some day my own camp would be a reality.

My lifelong hunting buddy, Dennis Obrien, and I happened on to the property in 1984. As partners, we purchased the acreage from the owner with a 10-year note. We built a camp and have enjoyed many great hunts. The best memories are of my two sons' first bow kills and of the heritage I have passed on to them. Camp time is the highlight of our year and hopefully for many to come.

It Sure Beats a Lean-To

Nancy Manning
Northboro, MA

In 1989, my husband, Cort, and I purchased almost 11 acres of land in the Adirondacks of New York. It was all thick woods. We bought it with the intention of "some day" building a camp. Cart, who is an avid hunter, our three children, then aged 5, 6 and 12, and I had been camping for years. We both work hard but there never seemed to be enough money to start building our camp. So every spring we would build a lean-to out of small trees and tarps, put the tents under the lean-to and in the summer we would camp. In the fall, my husband and his hunting buddies made the lean-to into "deer camp." No matter what the weather was—rain, snow and whatever else came along—they would never miss a hunting season. They would cook on a fireplace that they made out of cinder blocks. I remember the time he told me they went to cook breakfast, and when he went to crack the egg, it was frozen!

Anyway, little by little and tree by tree our family cleared a good-sized piece of land. Also Cort started saving things. He helped a friend take down a porch, and he saved the windows. He helped someone else remove a deck so they could build a bigger one, so he saved the old deck. He was given a wood stove that was all rust and he refinished it. Our cellar was starting to look like a flea market. You know the old saying "everything but the kitchen sink," well we had that too!

Each year the guys would go hunting, deer were taken and always the offer came, "If you ever need help building your camp, just let me know." In 1996, the offer the guys had made was called on. Each one of them and their wives or girlfriends came through. One weekend was for pouring cement, one for framing, one for roofing, and so on. And this was no short trip. Each way was 225 miles. The weather didn't always cooperate, but our friends did. We finally had the camp that we had dreamed of for so long. The inside is far from finished, but I'm happy to be able to close the front door.

So then we needed a name. Everyone has a name for their camp. We thought and thought and nothing seemed to fit. Then one day as we were getting ready to go home, a man came driving down our small dirt road. He stopped and introduced himself as the former owner of all the land before it was subdivided. He said he liked to take rides once in a while to look back on what he once had. So we invited him in to show him our camp-in-progress. As he was leaving, he and Cort shook hands, he got in his truck, he turned and looked back at our camp and said, "it sure beats a lean-to" and drove off. Cort and I looked at each other and knew we had the name for our camp …

Hunting Cottage

Andrew Anderson
Green Bay, WI

The "Country Club" people who have not visited our place graciously refer to it as a "cottage." It ranks as a pretty nice shack or a pretty shabby cabin. It's located far enough from the road that the whippoorwills are the most serious threat to a good night's sleep.

We built this camp two years ago. It took us a total of four days to build, with the hunting season being two weeks away. We have no electricity (not yet), just gas lights. Water is pumped by hand. A wood stove is our heat for those cold November hunting trips. Many hunting stories are shared with fellow hunters around the fire pit. It's a place we call home for the weekends. It has been the focal point of more fun and good memories than any group of guys could fairly expect. 🌲

South Florida Deer Camp

John Perez
Boca Raton, FL

This is our camp in South Florida. We made it out of an old moving truck that we bought for $300. We added a 12' x 20' screened porch for those South Florida mosquitoes. We can hunt ducks, quail, Osceola turkeys, deer, hogs, snipe and doves steps from our camp. It sleeps about 8 guys comfortably.

Nifty Fifty Camp

Ray Rheam
Millerstown, PA

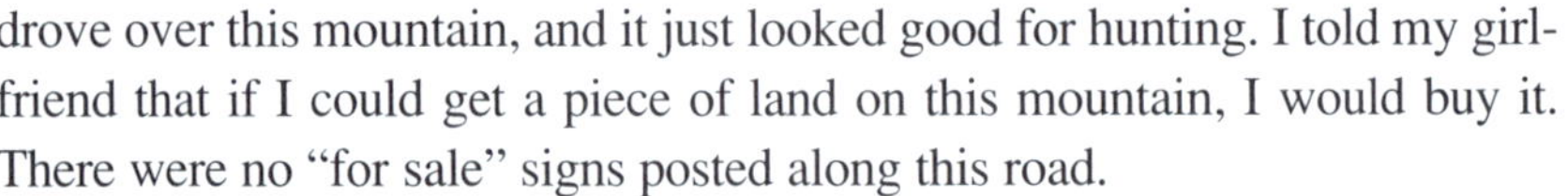

In 1992, my girlfriend and I decided to buy a piece of land in West Virginia, 250 miles away from home in Millerstown, Pennsylvania. On the way to the realty office in the town of Hundred, we got side tracked (or maybe most people call it lost). Well, we drove over this mountain, and it just looked good for hunting. I told my girlfriend that if I could get a piece of land on this mountain, I would buy it. There were no "for sale" signs posted along this road.

On the way to the realty office in the town of Hundred, we passed another realtor with a sign in his front lawn; unbeknownst to me, we would end up back there. When we got to the town of Hundred, the office was closed. So in the pouring down rain we headed back on Route 7 to the sign in the yard: "Blue Mt. Realty." We met George there and told him what we were looking for, asking him if he had anything listed with about 50 acres. Off we went with George to 2 different locations, but neither was quite what we wanted. He then said he had one other piece but that the property is hunted hard. I am from an area that has constant hunting pressure; I know what that's all about, so I said, "let's go look at it."

This is where the dream comes true. He took us back up to where we got lost. On the same mountain where I had said I'd like to buy, he pulled onto an old dirt road and went a half mile and said, "this is it." The 53 acres border 1000 acres of coal company ground. I could not believe it.

The name of the mountain is Klondike. Almost like the early gold rush days, when settlers went in to Alaska, I found my pot of gold in West Virginia. I told George right then that I'd buy it, but he wouldn't sell it to me that day; he said to go home and think on it. But I had my mind set already—this was the land for me. I called George the next day and told him to get the paper-

112

work done and that I wanted it.

For hunting pressure, there is none. Other than the 12 members of the camp, you will not see 10 other people hunting during the entire 3-month season.

The camp started out at 12' x 20', now it is 22' x 32'; we built on 3 times since 1992. The camp has no power to it, so we bought a generator for light and TV. We buried a 250-gallon tank for water, which we catch off the roof when it rains. We have a gas stove and refrigerator. So really, we have all the comforts of home and still rough it a little.

We have killed many deer over the years—110 to be exact: 46 bucks and 64 does. All the deer antlers are on the living room wall; we made a complete circle around a 12' x 20' room.

The members of the Nifty-Fifty Camp all hunt multiple seasons, of archery, rifle, and muzzleloader (muzzleloader being the best). Muzzleloader is the last season and it is not uncommon to shoot a buck then. For someone who likes to hunt, West Virginia offers a lot. They have a liberal hunting season and you can buy extra tags, so it's not one and done.

Our members range in age from a 70+ old man to a 20-year old whippersnapper. Do not let that 70-year old man fool you; he can go with the best of us, and he's the best turkey hunter we've got. Our occupations range from retired taxidermist to construction worker to artificial breeder. We even have a guy who makes artificial eyes for a living. What a mixed bag! But it's the nicest bunch you will ever want in hunting camp. We all feel it's not whether you kill something, it's just to get away from the rat race at home and enjoy what God put here on earth. Happy Trails.

Blood, Sweat & Tears

Dennis A. Janzen
Slinger, WI

It started in the spring of 1993 when we bought 40 acres of land, primarily for hunting. The land had an old trailer house on it that was pretty beat up. We decided that with a little fixing up, it would be good enough for our hunting camp … until one night we were playing cards and it started to rain. We got as wet inside as we would have if we had been out in our treestands.

We decided then and there to build ourselves a log cabin. We went into it without a clue of what we were doing. One of our partners had experience with house building but knew nothing about building a log house. We made arrangements to have the logs delivered and the concrete slab poured without even the slightest plans. We just went at it. We started in May with the help and support from family and friends working every weekend until hunting season. It took a lot of blood, sweat and tears (mostly from hitting our thumbs while roofing), but we finished in time to enjoy our first hunting season in our new log hunting shack.

Although there is not much tradition yet, we are looking forward to many years of building new traditions in our new hunting camp.

Diamond-in-the-Rough

Troy DeHart
Columbus, OH
Life Member

Outside, a cold blustery wind howls while inside, we are warm, dry and comfortable. As the rain beats a tattoo on our metal roof, sleep is inevitable.

All hunters dream of owning their own sanctuary, hunting without worry of trespass to infringe upon the enjoyment of their sport. This dream is by three hunting friends: Ray Maddox, George Griffith and I.

We three, through the drive of Ray, who died in a hunting-related accident in 1992 and to whom our hunting cabin is dedicated, embarked on a pursuit of a piece of land to suit our dreams. With amazing luck, in 1991, we were able to purchase 30+ acres surrounded by Wayne National Forest.

After Ray's untimely death, George, a close personal friend named Gary Cordle, and I set out to finish our dream. Thanks to many, and particularly to Jerry L. Miller of Huston Construction Company of Columbus, Ohio.

Our core group of 10 hunters is supplemented by upwards of 20 others during bow, shotgun, primitive weapon, squirrel, rabbit and grouse.

Because we want to continue the hunting tradition, we ask that folks bring their children or borrow one or two and bring them along. This past year, we had 10 young men under the age of 18—two of them first-time hunters— who enjoyed Diamond-in-the-Rough. There have been several women and young ladies who have enjoyed Diamond-in-the-Rough and its available activities: hunting, swimming, fishing, hiking, trapping, camping, ATV riding, cutting firewood and more.

1956

Thomas Varbero
Harrison, NY

As you see, the picture enclosed is my log cabin built by myself in 1956. It's an unusual log cabin. What I mean is that the logs I used are unusual. There was a lumber mill nearby that cut veneer sheet of oak trees cut 9 feet long. The 9-foot long log would go into a steam room for weeks at a time until the log was soft enough to cut the paper-thin veneer that was used for furniture.

The cutting would stop when it got down to the last 8 or 10 inches of the center of the large log. The waste piece would be a solid oak log 9 feet long by 8 or 10 inches. I first cut them for firewood, then I started building my log cabin.

I used 2 logs to start end for end to make it 18 feet long by 9 feet wide. 9-foot oak log is very heavy. The last few on top I pulled up with my 1930 Model A Ford pickup (named Nellie Belle).

Inside were 4 bunk beds, a stove (gas) to cook, a potbelly stove for heat, a table and 4 chairs. Windows and door were picked up curbside from a house that was installing new ones. Roofing was from crating material that a factory disposed of curbside also. It's still going strong, and many times I let NAHC members use it when I'm away.

Deer, bear and lots of turkeys could be taken right from the front porch. I usually close it up in December and go back again in April to have a look-see. Then, turkey hunting in May.

Lights were with propane gas; now I have electricity after 30 years. Water was taken up; now I have a well. Toilets are flushed with a bucket of water.

The log cabin is a mile up from the gravel dirt road. I used to park my car then drive the Model A pickup to my camp, using a full set of chains and driving it in first gear—even after it sat around for 2 or 3 months, I would just prime it 3 or 4 times and it would start right up. I cut out the floor over the muffler for heat inside the pickup. After I got my first 4 x 4, a NAHC member saw the Model A parked near the log cabin and I sold it to him for $75. After a few years I wished I had it back (to restore). 🌲

Harris Mountain Cabin

Jerry L. Windle
Livingston, TN

I built the cabin in 1992 after retiring. The cabin is located on Harris Mountain in Overton County on 200 acres of land that I own and where I, along with my family, hunt each season.

We have harvested many deer from this location; the best to date being a nice 12-point last November. Also this year were three 8-point and two 6-point deer.

The outside of the cabin is made of hemlock and the inside red cedar. There's one bedroom downstairs and one upstairs. The stove and refrigerator are both propane. The cabin is heated by a wood burning stove, the electricity is furnished by a generator and water is furnished by a spring that is gravity-fed to the cabin.

Other game on this location include turkey, grouse, quail, squirrel, rabbit, coon, opossum, bobcat and coyote.

The Ranch

Ralph J. Bridge
Stamford, CT
Life Member

The completion of our deer shack on our "Ranch," as we call it, took us six years from ground breaking to the staining of the deck last August. It was the earnest desire of me, my brother-in-law, Tom, and my dad (Ken Sr.) … and a lifelong dream come true.

After searching Connecticut, Maine, and New York for a piece of country land to buy, we finally pooled funds and invested in over 100 acres in the Catskill Mountains of New York state. We subsequently created many long trails, 2 multi-acre fields, rifle and archery ranges, 7 treestands, a large stone patio/campsite with a great fireplace and our 8- x 16- foot cabin with its 10- x 20- foot deck, through hundreds of labor hours over the years.

The leaky old tent and sleeping bags we started with gave way to a deteriorating old pop-up trailer we towed from Rhode Island. Plans were drawn up and tools and materials were hauled over 200 miles for countless trips for the years of construction. About the time of the trailer's demise, we were able to start using the new cabin before its completion. Although the cabin is fully

The cabin before adding the deck off the front. The old pine "Country Farm Home" sign came from the dump!

wired and insulated, we have no electricity, water or plumbing. Inside, we have two lofts that sleep two each, an old Castro convertible for two more and lots of floor space for sleeping bags. The walls were done in old sanded- and light-stained barn boards. The two doors, deck and ramp make wheelchair access easy.

Three generations of Bridge family members and our friends have derived much enjoyment from our Ranch, and we have given it many devoted hours of work. The children are thrilled with the coyote's scary howling and the owl's eerie hooting under the dark night's starry sky. The kids roast hot dogs and toast marshmallows over the bright wood fire in the nighttime darkness of the forest setting. The good fortune of success- ful annual deer and turkey harvests, blueber- ry picking and occasional bear sightings are among our treasures.

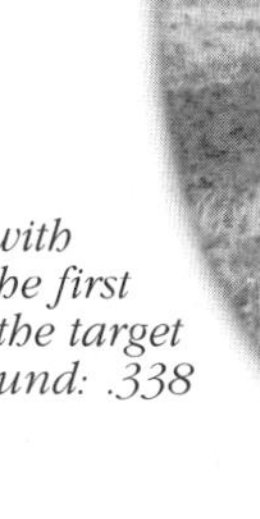

Ralph Bridge and his dad, Ken, with Ralph's doe. "I shot clear across the first field into the second one behind the target range—about 140 yards. One round: .338 Browning Semi Automatic."

East Canada Creek

Jerry Gregoire
Cohoes, NY

In 1994, I purchased the land on East Canada Creek in Fulton County. The following year I built a small hunting camp: 12' x 16'.

There are four of us who hunt the land: James Akley Sr., James Akley Jr., Ed Sherman and me. We've been hunting together for over 15 years.

In 1995, James Jr. took the first deer. In 1996, I took the first buck during black powder season and the second doe in 1997 with black powder.

This isn't the hottest spot in New York, but it's our favorite because it's ours.

The Valley of Ghosts Camp

Harvey Yeager
Rice Lake, WI

Our little hunting cabin is in the heart of the Blue Hills region east of Rice Lake, Wisconsin. It has been on site since 1994 deer hunting season. We call the cabin The Valley of Ghosts Camp. The name comes from the long-ago loggers in the area who called a huge felsemeer canyon close to the cabin Valley of Ghosts—named from wind moaning through the rocks. The whole area is a series of hardwood—poplar, second-growth poplar and spruce swamp mixed in with sharp ridges and valleys with a trout stream cutting through the property. Ideal deer woods. Most seasons our little group fills all tags the first weekend of the season.

One landmark close to camp is the long-abandoned village of the horseman. It was once a stagecoach stop-over complete with blacksmith, hotel, post office, trading post, tavern and a band of Chippewa Indians with tepees. And also close by is a large felsemeer canyon protected by the state of Wisconsin—one of only a handful of true felsemeers. Truly beautiful country.

The best part of the hunting and cabin existence is how it all came together. This simple co-existence between landowner and outdoorsman should be first on all guests' minds. Remember, as outsiders we are guests on privately owned lands. I had hunted this farmer's property for about 25 years. Each year for Christmas, New Year's or Easter I would buy a large turkey or ham to show appreciation for allowing me access. Then during the summer of 1994 I got the bug to hunt out of a cabin. I drew up plans and papers, went to the farmer with my plans and a nominal yearly fee for cabin site and hunting. And just because I had shown him that I was a caring and responsible hunter, by golly, he said to go ahead and put it all together.

The cabin is a full ¾ mile off the road on an old logging road. Far enough in so no one bothers it, and it has a true feeling of being "back in." For as long as it lasts, it's a good situation all the way around. 🌲

Camp Makwa

Clare Seidel
Reading, PA

Our camp was built in 1995 by my wife and me, along with sweat, muscle and know-how from our friends. We acquired a local excavator, brick layer, electrician and plumber. The cabin was designed by John, our mentor, a friend of many years, a hunter and an NAHC member. Having the foundation and floor in place, we built the exterior walls. The open beam ceiling was installed using ladders, scaffolding, pullies and muscles. We had it under roof in 10 days. We added the decks the following year.

Our cabin, Camp Makwa, is located in Tioga County, Pennsylvania. Makwa, Canadian Inuit, means black bear. We have black bear, sometimes with cubs, visit and also deer and turkey.

On occasion you may hear coyotes. An annual coyote hunt for Tioga and Lycoming Counties is a hunt I enjoy. The hunt is organized by local hunters,

hunters sign up at Inn 287, where food and lodging is available. Hunting with the local hunters gives me the chance to hunt in new areas and make new friends.

My wife and I head for camp the Wednesday before Thanksgiving, sharing the holiday with friends. We stay for the first week of buck season. Fellow hunters arrive Saturday and treestands are set up. Saturday night is card playing. Monday night we visit Camp Caribou for dinner and to share our first day of buck experience with friends.

We spend 90-plus days a year at camp. Most of the days are weekend visits, summer vacation, holidays, and, of course, hunting season. Arriving after a 3-hour drive I always say to my wife, "Honey, we're home."

Siskiyou County: Blacktail Camp

Callan Payton
Beckwourth, CA

What makes my deer camp cabin so unique is that I built it all myself using no electricity: here in the heart of black-tailed deer country, in Siskiyou County, California. But the lumber is southern pine I logged and had sawed into boards in Arkansas and hauled out here when I moved back. The cabin was built in about 1 year; I started in 1996.

I killed a forkhorn buck that fall and saw the biggest record-book blacktail I've ever seen.

It's my hunting cabin, trophy room and weekend retreat all combined. And hopefully, the beginning of a lot of memories and hunting heritage for my 12-year-old son who helped me build it. In short, it's a dream come true in prime black bear, blacktail deer, steelhead and salmon and gold-panning country. 🌲

West Lake Ainslie

Walter Furdas
Sydney, Nova Scotia, Canada

My camp is located on 300 acres (which I own) in the West Lake Ainslie area of Inverness County in Cape Breton, Nova Scotia. Although the camp is located on 300 acres, we hunt several thousand acres, which consist of neighboring properties that we have permission to hunt on. The land is gentle rolling land and consists mostly of mature evergreens (pine, spruce and fir.). There are some cut-overs, and the bulk of the property consists of agricultural fields.

The cabin is approximately 24' x 16' and consists of a bedroom (with 4 bunks), a living room with fold-out bunk and cot, and a kitchen area. There are 3 stoves in the cabin, 2 in the living room area; these being an oil stove and a combination wood/coal stove. There is also a propane stove in the kitchen area that we use for cooking. We have a sink in the kitchen area too. In the addition to the cabin, which is approximately 14' x 18', we have a shower, toilet and vanity.

There is no power to the cabin and lighting is provided by Coleman lanterns. Water used for drinking is carried in and rainwater is used for showering and flushing. We have plans to install a veranda on the front of the cabin to take in the beautiful view of Lake Ainslie.

I have had the cabin now for 9 years, and there are 5 other hunters who hunt out of this location. However, last year there have only been 2 or 3 of us at the camp at any one time.

Game consists of white-tailed deer, bear, coyote, rabbit, grouse and pheasant (not plentiful), ducks and geese. Moose hunting is by draw only and is only minutes away from the camp, although there has been the occasional sighting near the camp.

Lake Ainslie offers excellent trout fishing, and the Mergoree River and the Bros D'or Lake which is only minutes away offer excellent trout and salmon fishing. The Bros D'or Lake also offers cod, mackerel and the occasional halibut.

Scandinavian Cabin

Frank Bolyard
Flemington, WV

We built our cabin in the fall of 1991. I came from a large family of seven boys and one girl. As we began to the move away from home, we realized that we needed a place to gather in the fall to continue our hunting traditions.

My wife, Shawn, and I decided to build a cabin on the back side of my father's 250 acre farm, as we also had permission to hunt on about 3,000 acres of timber company land that bordered that side of the property. I then went to the local library and found a book explaining the "Scandinavian" method of building a log cabin.

As Shawn peeled the bark from the 22' x 12" poplar logs with a draw knife, I trimmed and fit them together on the walls. Our daughter Misty and son Luke helped also to make it a family project. When we reached the top of the walls and the 32' long perlins, some of my brothers joined in and helped with the roof and floor. We sawed what lumber we needed

on the family farm sawmill and the shingles were donated from leftover odd jobs to give the roof a "camo" look. We finished the project with about $250 and a lot of sweat invested.

Today the cabin is used by family and friends alike as the door is never locked and everyone is welcome. In the years past, we have never had anything stolen or vandalized, unless you include the bear that took a bite out of the cooler or the bear that hibernated "under" the cabin one winter.

Every weekend, holiday, or anytime we get a chance from October through December each year, my son Luke and I spend at the cabin. We never know who will be there, but we know we will have a good time.

We are building memories every year, from Luke's first deer to the big 10-point buck my brother Doug shot behind the big rock stand or the time I put salt in the kool-aid instead of sugar or the time my brother Brian brought his father-in-law up to hunt (If anyone ever insists on sleeping in their truck because they snore, don't try to convince them otherwise). We remember all these stories and more and tell them over and over year after year to the delight of young and old alike. And that is how we are continuing our hunting traditions. 🌲

Big Twin Creeks

James Sullivan
Highland Heights, KY
Life member

Enclosed are a few pictures of our deer camp. The property is owned by member Martin McCabe. He has 125 acres of hardwood and cedar trees. The property is located in Owen County, Kentucky. It is bordered on all sides by other farms in the county. It also has 2 creeks running through it. That is how it got its name as Big Twin Creeks. The property has been owned by "Marty" for over 20 years.

I have never seen Marty turn anyone down if they ask if they can hunt. Marty is a very conscientious man when it comes to taking care of the property. We have trails all around the property that we have cut so we can ride our ATVs when we are not hunting. We also provide the animals with grain and salt.

This is the first year for our cabin. Before then we slept in our trucks, some with truck caps, others with just a tarp thrown over the back to keep the weather off of them.

The cabin was built this year by Marty McCabe and me. The products used were all leftover products from several sub-contractors; or products were purchased from a home improvement store/lumberyard as "non-saleable material." One of our hunting pals supplied shingles left over from a garage project, the windows were from a replacement job of mine; all I had to do was build a frame for them. The floor is all treated lumber 2 x 4's, 2 x 6's, 2 x 8's and 2 x 10's. The units were ones that nobody could sell. They were warped, split or ones that nobody wanted to purchase for one reason or another. The siding was donated by another hunting pal of ours. The T-111 for the walls was purchased from a home supply store going out of business. Our front porch is not quite finished yet, but we will finish it before hunting season gets here.

It took several weekends to build, but it was well worth it. We have no modern conveniences like electricity or running water, but it sure is a lot better than sleeping in our trucks.

We do have Coleman lanterns, a permanent sink taken out of a house being remodeled, and a portable stove. I also have been granted life-long hunting permission by Marty. If not for him and his good nature, this would not have been possible. Thanks, Marty.

A New Hampshire Deer Camp

Frank Fisk
Keene, NH

Our camp—in the town of Washington, New Hampshire,—was built in 1985; we used all rough pine natural lumber. We own 25 acres, but there are many more acres here to hunt on. Deer here are not real big bucks, but our camp is good for a couple good whitetails per year. We sure do have a lot for happy hours trying, and many good meals are cooked here on the wood stove.

Split Water Deer Camp

Richard J. Carr
Detroit Lakes, MN

Our deer camp is located in Becker County near the south shore of Shell Lake. We named our camp Split Water Deer Camp because there is a water divide that runs through our land with the snow melt and rain on the east side flowing to the Mississippi and on the west side flowing into the Red River and going north into Canada.

The "shack" as we call it is a 40 x 60 pole barn that was taken apart and moved to our site piece by little piece. We have a "great room," an indoor bathroom and sauna, four bedrooms (which sleep 12 to 16) and a drive-through garage storage area.

We mainly hunt whitetails but have hunted black bear, ducks and geese, and there are lots of grouse along our trails.

The best part is the deer camp aspect. The four of us who own the camp all have sons, and it is so great to see everyone pulling into camp on the Friday before season, all the stories and changes; the "first deer-biggest deer pots" and just the general overall camaraderie that fills the camp as more people arrive. We have no third generation hunters in our camp yet, but I look to that day; also to the day that we get some female hunters in our camp. I would really enjoy having one of my granddaughters to hunt with.

The food is always good, the coffee always hot and the wood stove keeps the place warm. We do use it year around, cross-country skiing in the winter. It's a real treat to see the pristine snow and hear the wind whispering through the big old 100' pines we have on the property, some next to the "shack."

Chalet Hunting Camp

Carl Martin
East Earl, PA

In 1980, we built this deer hunting camp on 10 acres of mountain ground in Huntingdon County, Pennsylvania. We heard about an old farm house that was built in the Weaverland Valley by the first Mennonite settlers coming into the Lancaster County area. The historians wanted to preserve the old house, but it was in the area of an expanding stone quarry. My brother John, a partner in our cabin and employee of the stone quarry, managed to get us first pick of the old oak joist and rafters that we left exposed in our rustic cabin. When agreements were reached to allow the removal of the old stone house, we quickly rented a truck and took out what we needed and took the load of timber 130 miles west to the 10 acres we had recently purchased.

We had family who wanted to become members of our camp, so we asked them to give 40 hours of labor helping to build the cabin to give them membership. They agreed, and the first year we had 14 hunters.

After a couple years of hunting, we realized we located in an excellent area. This past year with 12 hunters, we harvested 8 bucks and 4 does, and to date we have harvested a total of 120 white-tailed deer.

Yes, building a cabin on vacation days and Saturdays was a lot of hard work, but with the help of others that are members now, together we have many good times working, vacationing and hunting in Huntingdon County, Pennsylvania. 

Trails End

Ken Skrivan
Endwell, NY

It was built from its own property. Has a nice, big wood stove to keep us toasty. Sleeps about nine. Oh, did I mention we have carpet and a microwave? There are a lot of memories involved in the years that will never be forgotten. Also, many "unbelievable" stories.

Loggers Lodge

Rodger A. Laughman
Spring Grove, PA

Our deer camp was built in 1988, but our deer hunting tradition is quite a bit older. I remember in 1961 when I was sixteen, going along with my dad to hunt around our home in the Pidgeon Hills of York County, Pennsylvania.

I built this camp in northern Potter County, Pennsylvania, with the help of family and friends. I sawed all of the material possible at my sawmill, everything from the outside siding to the open beam ceiling. We named it Loggers Lodge. The small shed you see in the background of the photo was our camp until we got our main camp built.

Our deer hunting has these same friends and family sharing and enjoying what we built. From the older guys who snore to the third generation starting to hunt. Our trophy wall consists of horns on plaques, shirt tails, a couple of impressive heads and pictures plus a picture of Dad with a buck, the man who started all of these great times. This camp would not have been possible without the help of my wife, Betty, and two sons Dave and Jeb. We spent long days, drove lots of miles north and worked up a lot of sweat, but they hung in until it was finished.

East Mountain Camp

Brett Torrey
Manchester Center, VT

The East Mountain Camp, as it's known around Manchester, Vermont, is located in the heart of the Green Mountain National Forest on a plot of land that my parents gave to me about six years ago. Four good friends and I got together, pooled our labor time, and built this 16 x 36 two-room cabin.

It is about one mile in from the town road by 4 x 4 or by foot and it sits on seventeen acres. Fully finished off inside, we can comfortably sleep about ten people. Heated by wood, lit and cooked by gas, there's an outhouse in the back and 20 gallon water tank that sits next to the sink.

We hunt whitetails, turkeys, partridge, mostly and about 300 yards from camp we have a river called Bourne Brook that runs out of Bourne Pond, which this supplies us with some nice swimming and trout fishing.

The Above-Ground Hunting Camp

Robert Porter
Davis, WV
Life Member

Welcome to one of our two treehouse hunting camps that we use to spot and hunt game from in the swamps of Canaan Valley in Tucker County, West Virginia. Most of our work was done on weekends with one ladder, a farm tractor with front-end loader, and pulleys and ropes.

Here's a little history from the oldest treehouse camp, called T1. It was built almost 20 years ago by some of my older brother-in-laws with a brainstorming idea to be able to watch the whole swamp. A lot of nice whitetail bucks that were taken in the swamp were spotted from it. It has a wood/coal stove, one bed stand and six windows. We also use it for camping during warmer weather.

Now a little about the one in the picture, called T2. As the hardhacks and hawthorne brush grew over the years, visibility and spotting distance dwindled. So, in 1997 we decided to build another treehouse. We picked a location, and in the spring of 1998 we set the poles. The floor was built in the air around the poles, then the walls were built on the ground and pulled up and set into place. My nephew, being the young and fearless teenager, finished putting the roof on himself. Then he climbed over the side and let himself in one of the windows. (I thought his mom would kill us for letting him do this.)

T2 is about twice the size of the old treehouse; its dimensions are 11 1/2' x 11 1/2' and it sits 23 feet off the ground. It also has a wood/coal stove, one bed stand, a fold down wall mounted bed on the highest front wall, and four windows.

When the season begins, we usually go in on Sunday and stay in T1 and T2 until Tuesday, then we go in early in the morning for the rest of the sea-

son. Our first year in T2 was a good year, we took deer from both this camp and T1. I would also like to mention that one of our new younger hunters killed his first deer this year. Spotted from T1, it was a nice 8-point with a 19½ inch spread. 🌲

Handmade Camp

Dave Lewis
Erie, PA

Camp owners: Dave and Carolyn Lewis

Location: Warren County in northwestern Pennsylvania.

Nearest towns: Titusville and Grand Valley.

History: The building of the camp was started in 1988 and took approximately 5 years to complete.

All logs used in the camp came from the six acres which the camp sits on. All of the logs (approximately 65) were cut down by hand using either ax or chain saw and were dragged to the site either by hand or with help from a tractor. Then all the logs were handed-peeled with draw knives and screw drivers, then notched by hand and lifted into place on the walls either by hand or with the help from a chain fall.

The gaps between the logs were filled and sealed with

chimney mortar, but first, thousands of nails were driven in at angles to give the mortar something to grip to.

There is electricity at the cabin, heat is provided with a wood stove, water is carried in, and a good old-fashioned outhouse is in use.

The camp is used year 'round, almost every weekend.

The Risewick Deer Camp

Jack Risewick
Rochester, NY

The Risewick Deer Camp is a 24' x 32' 2-story, modified A-frame building located on 6 acres of land in the town of Caneadea in Allegany County, New York. Our global address is 43 deg. 22' 17" north latitude by 78 deg. 10' 22" west longitude at an elevation of 1667 feet. above sea level. Originally, we purchased a 2-acre property in January of 1973 that bordered on approximately 1500 acres of state land. Since the A-frame was built in 1990, we have acquired an additional 4 acres to increase our holding to the current 6-acre tract.

During the early years of ownership, we purchased a used 19' trailer and located that on the 2-acre site. This served us well for many years as a home-base during the deer hunting season. As my sons reached the age where they could legally hunt, the trailer still provided adequate space. In the late 1980s, they began to ask if a friend or two might join us. At this time we decided to build a hunting camp.

I had been in several A-frames and decided that this was the type of place I wanted. I had noted a few drawbacks at some of these cabins (small kitchens, small bathrooms, and some exterior deterioration due to moisture being absorbed into the lower edges of the roof structure.) These concerns caused me to decide on a modified A-frame design. We would have a small pitched roof at the peak before going into the standard A-frame look. In addition, the building would be built on a cinder block foundation approximately 38" above ground level. At the entry end, we would incorporate an 8' x 10' air lock. This feature would serve as a point of entry and would allow for the removal of wet or muddy boots prior to entering the house proper. In addition, this area would be home for the hot water heater, double laundry tubs, and the electrical breaker box.

The camp is heated by a Quadra-fire wood burning stove that is positioned diagonally opposite of the stairs that lead to the second level. The centrally located paddle fan helps to keep the heat from rising to the first level ceiling while the stair opening creates a chimney effect that draws the warm air to the second level, where a second centrally located paddle fan forces the air downward into the main sleeping quarters.

The entire inside was finished off by using 1" x 6" knotty pine tongue-and-groove planking. To be precise, the cabin is finished with 1.0727 miles of knotty pine planking.

We can trace ownership of this land back to 1863. This has served as an inspiration for us to make log entries each year so that future Risewicks can read what happened at any given time as we continue to develop the properties.

Current activities include turning two acres into a Black Walnut tree plantation. And a section that receives an abundance of sunlight has been designated as the location where we will attempt to plant a section of sweet corn.

Although the properties have been recently logged, we plant more trees than we remove. Two years ago, we planted a number of apple trees on the backside of the original two acres where the A-frame is located. Some skeptics told us that the deer would eat the apple saplings. We have attached two 35 mm film canisters on each tree. One is filled with shavings of a deodorant soap and the other contains moth balls. To date, we have not had damage to the trees and in only their second year, two yellow delicious apple trees bore fruit. We have seen deer tracks in the snow leading up to the trees and then noticed that once close, the deer turn and walk away from the mini-orchard.

A unique feature of this camp relates to the importance we place on hunter safety. I carefully screen any new hunting partners to assure that they behave in a manner that places personal safety first. In addition, those who come to our camp as invited guests during the hunting season complete a form that includes name, age, next of kin along with appropriate phone numbers, primary physician's name and phone number, a listing of any medications to which one might be allergic, and finally, the name and number of their health care insurance provider. Heaven forbid that we ever need any of this information, but if we do, it is available.

One-Room Shack

Robert J. Manske
Portage, WI
Life Member

Here is our deer camp in Wisconsin. Our one room shack is far from fancy, but it is warm and dry. It's a great place to eat lunch, warm up, or watch a football game while still being able to see deer through the window. Many deer have been shot out in front of our little shack, and when a nice buck comes running across the field, you should see 5 people trying to fit out a 3-foot door.

Our shack was started and built around 1978 with wood from a torn down building and some old windows. We acquired an old wood stove, a used kitchen stove and some very used furniture with which to furnish our small shack. We "sided" our place with rolled tar paper left over from someone's roofing project. As the years went by, we upgraded our shack. We added some Styrofoam sheets for insulation, some leftover paneling for the walls and a used piece of carpeting for the floor. We eventually took out the wood stove and replaced it with a kerosene heater—it was cleaner, easier and faster. We even upgraded the furniture—whatever family and friends were willing to give to us.

Our shack is used by my father, brother, a few uncles and cousins, and of course, myself. Occasionally, neighbors stop by to visit and see how the hunt is going, as well as to sit and watch the Thanksgiving football game. It is amazing how may people fit around a 6-inch television set.

Sometimes we bring the pop-up camper and park it by the shack. It is portable and it's a nice place to sleep, but it lacks the room, comfort and tradition of our shack.

CHAPTER four

A Family Affair

If you're like most hunters, your first memory of deer camp is a special one. Maybe you recall being curled up under the blankets in nervous sleepless anticipation of Opening Morning. Or perhaps you remember Dad placing you in a treestand ... and then never imagining that a sunrise could be so magical. And cold! The one constant in any first-hunt memory is family. Because even if the person who first brought you hunting wasn't immediate family, he or she immediately *became* family. In fact, almost all deer camp memories are that way; they're made special by the people we're with on those precious, wonderful days in camp.

The Jacob Farm

Russell Ux
Douglassville, PA

When you say the words "deer camp" a wide variety of interpretations can come to mind. Ours really isn't a camp in the true sense of the word, but it still is steeped in the traditions and camaraderie of other deer camps. We hunt on The Jacob Farm, a 200 acre Pennsylvania dairy farm.

Let me tell you, there is nothing like hunting farmland deer; it's a little different than in the deep woods, but we do also hunt the woods surrounding the farm. There are four of us—call us diehards who hunt the farm all the time—bow season, the gun season and small game. These fine fellows include George Jacob III, who grew up on the farm and knows it like the back of his hand—he recently took a nice 10-point buck on the farm this year; Mike Heydt, a guy who seems to have a sixth sense when it comes to deer hunting—always knowing where the deer are going to be, and being able to be in the right place at the right time; Kim Burns, George's brother-in-law, who always seems to have a joke or funny story to tell to pass the

time when we are sitting on stand and there isn't much deer action; and me, Russell Ux, the newest member of the bunch.

I can't begin to tell you all of the memories and good times we have had hunting on the farm. I, myself, feel fortunate to have such great friends as these guys and to be able to hunt at such a great place as The Jacob Farm.

Thank you to my buddies, who let me share in and help make such great memories. If you are a person who likes to hunt or who enjoys the outdoors, you will know what I mean.

Deer Yard Camp

Dan Dussault
Danville, VT

Each fall as the vibrant col-ored leaves fall to the earth's floor, members of the Deer Yard Camp head north for the tradi-tional opening weekend of Vermont's deer season. Deer Yard Camp is located in the northeastern corner of Vermont known to most as "The Northeast Kingdom." It is here where we begin our quest in search of the elusive whitetail. The Northeast Kingdom is known for its larger bodied deer; however, it does not hold the mass numbers of white-tails compared to other areas in Vermont and surrounding New England states. The serenity and peacefulness of the big woods brings a certain emotion to all who hunt here.

Camp members include co-owner and camp commander, my father, Andre "The Professor" Dussault, (also, co-owner and not to be forgotten, my mother, Gertrude Dussault); Dick "The Bald Eagle" Bedor (known to all as the most valuable camp hand); myself, Dan "The Adjuster" Dussault; brothers-in-law, George "the Caster" Desorcie and Kevin "Jardine" Biggie; and lastly, my best friend, Mike "Hardwood" Hemond Jr.

Deer Yard Camp was established in 1984 as my father's vision to be a place where hunters and good friends gather to share old memories and make new ones. When we are rewarded with success, it is a tradition that evening for the proud hunter to illuminate the meat pole. This will allow all to view his trophy through the camp's picture window as he recounts his hunt.

To all deer camps across the country, may that big buck gliding through the hardwoods stop just as he enters your sights. Good huntin' from the Deer Yard Camp!

Overmyer Deer Camp

Leonard G. Overmyer III
Grand Rapids, MI

My young son represents the 10th generation of hunters in our family—a hunter's tradition that dates back to the Pennsylvania frontier days of the Revolutionary War. As later generations traveled westward, our branch of the Overmyer family eventually settled part of a wilderness setting in the Northern-Lower Peninsula of Michigan where at least 5 direct generations of my family have hunted. Our tree farm outside the small towns of Copemish and Mesick, Michigan, are just a few miles from where the 1998 World Record Whitetail is believed to have been taken.

Our belief in ethical hunting and conservation efforts to promote volunteer quality deer/wildlife management techniques with our neighbors has been an important part of our success.

Deer Camp in the Valley

Robin Wallin
New Berlin, WI

To get to our deer camp, you must first cross through the trout stream that flows in front of the property. Once you have crossed the river and climb a bank, you see the most beautifully maintained prairie fields that lead you to the base of a valley with oak ridge bluffs on both sides. Vance's (the landowner) fields have taken first place in a prairie field contest.

In addition to the beautiful surroundings, our camp consists of a teepee and an Amish, rustic-looking cabin. There is no electricity or running water. We use oil lanterns and a hand pump well. However, there is a hot tub located near the river that we fill with a pump that hooks up to a jeep that the landowner keeps there for this purpose. Vance is the kindest, most down-to-earth landowner that I have ever had the opportunity to meet, and

the 5 people who hunt his land are very thoughtful, kind and appreciative to him for all of his generosity. We can't thank him enough for the privilege to hunt on his land.

The enjoyment we find in nature and the heritage of our hunting (both archery and rifle), which has been turned down to us from our forefathers, will continue as we, in turn, share this legacy with our children.

Jesse and Hunter Locke's Boulder Lodge

Randy Locke
Waterville, VT
Life Member

Location: Codding Hollow Road, Waterville, Vermont. Built in 1997 by their Poppa, Dad, uncle and friends. Used for white-tailed deer hunting and weekend outings. Jesse is 5 years old; Hunter is 3 years old. 🌲

The Porubsky Cabin

Brad Porubsky
Topeka, KS

The Porubsky Cabin is located on Mill Creek, just east of Buffalo Mound in the Flint Hills of Kansas. Legends say that the Plains Indians used Buffalo Mound as a lookout for buffalo herds. Today, white-tailed deer and turkeys roam the Flint Hills and catfish swim Mill Creek. Four generations of Porubskys enjoy hunting and fishing the Flint Hills of Kansas; our cabin is truly our "home on the range."

The Gor-B-Inn

Scott F. Page
Lowell, MA

Just east of the Allegash wilderness and just west of tarred roads and electricity sits our hunting camp. It was built by section men on the Bangor and Aroostook Railroad for a Mr. Jerry Strout, who was president of the railroad. The men used horses to bring in boards from a boxcar for the flooring and roof. The remainder of the camp was finished with hand-cut logs.

The camp was bought by my grandparents, Emmett (Don) and Geneva Ross and my father, Frederick Page Jr., in 1956. The place was named after the friendly Canadian blue jays nicknamed "gorbys" that always appear looking for handouts while opening up camp.

In the early years of the camp, you had to pack in food, clothes and guns,

then hike about two miles through the woods. About halfway there, you had to wade across Fish River before continuing on. A few years later, logging roads and a bridge were put in just past the camp. A path was made that is still used today, well worn from many trips in and out.

A tradition my dad started after they bought the camp was to mount the lucky hunter's deer antlers on a plaque inscribed with their name and year of the shot. In the beginning, my grandfather chuckled at the idea, until the ceiling of the camp began to fill up with antlers from so many unlucky bucks. With every mount, came a storytelling session told around the table, which is still done to this day.

Another hunter from those early years is my father's good friend Ike Whitten who, like my dad, enjoys the outdoors. Ike and my father taught us young boys about gun safety and knowing your target. We learned how to read deer sign, how to look for and track them, how to handle the wounded ones and finally how to clean them. We were taught that hunting was not just about killing an animal but an adventure to be enjoyed by taking in all that nature had to offer along the way. We learned about that special bonding that only hunters know exists between fellow hunters.

The camp has been handed down to myself now as well as Ike's two boys, Bob and Mark Whitten and their brother-in-law, Robert Lambert. We have all hunted together here for over twenty years. The camp has seen its share of 200+ bucks and even placed 4th in the state of Maine for a non-typical shot by Bob in 1987. Some seasons we have no luck at all while others we get two or three.

I feel blessed to have had the opportunity to hunt with my grandparents as a boy. They are now no longer with us but live on in our hearts continually. All of their lives they enjoyed the hunting season to the fullest. I am also blessed to be able to hunt with some of the best people I know. I feel that a great deer camp is not only in being in the right spot or having the perfect terrain but also by those who pass through its doors.

I have two young boys of my own, Mike and Jeff, who excite me when I see that look in their eyes as we head to the camp. Though they are not old enough to deer hunt yet, I use the same lessons that I was taught by my elders—safety first, know your target and the rest will come later. I hope our children have the chance to enjoy this great sport as we have and start their own traditions within the camp. Our deer antler mounting tradition started by

father would now make my grandfather proud—we have filled the front half of the camp and have a good jump on the back end where the bunk beds are.

To those who enjoy hunting and fishing as much as we do, I hope you have a place that is special to your hunting party—and to the people I hunt with past, present and future, thank you for a lifetime of memories.

Virginia Memories

Kenneth Fuller
Meadowview, VA
Life Member

This is the camper my father and I hunted deer out of. It was on 100 acres in Buckingham County, Virginia. My father bought the land from a fellow police officer Larry Biddle when Larry retired.

My father hunted there from the early 1970s till his death in a car crash in 1996. I hunted with him on the land from 1986 till his death. I then hunted one more year till we sold the place.

We hunted with shotguns and dogs in that part of Virginia. The time spent in the camper and on that land with my father were some of the best times of my life.

History of Phantom Road Hunters, Inc.

Gerald Sabol
Duluth, MN

The camp of Phantom Road Hunters, Inc. is located in northwestern Minnesota 12 miles north of Grygla, Minnesota, or approximately 30 miles from the Canadian border. The hunters who began this camp started deer hunting this area as far back as 1949. After hunting the area for many years, they put together a core group of 15 hunters in 1968 and purchased an old log farmhouse nestled into a 160-acre quarter section. The land was incorporated as a non-profit entity and we celebrated our 30th anniversary this past fall.

The name Phantom Road Hunter was derived from an actual event, and the Phantom Buck mythology is legend among our group. We presently have

12 shareholders and hunt an average of 20 men per year from this shack. Our deer tally success ebbs and flows over the years due to harsh winters in this north country, wolf predation and agriculture crops.

Some of the traditions of Phantom Road Hunters are a Big Buck contest, the Eight Point Club and the Rear End Award with each one giving you special name recognition. The Big Buck contest winner receives money that is pooled every year. The Eight Point Club hunters have a picture of their animal mounted on a wall plaque along with an arm band stripe with the year they shot their buck for their hunting coat. The Rear End award is given to the hunter who screws up, which is a mount of a whitetail's rear end hanging in our camp with a brass name plate below it with the year of the incident. We also wear our corporate logo on our hunting coats and have special hunting caps made up with the logo or design on them.

An annual journal is created from daily notes with pictures and a pretty good story line about the particular conditions of that year. We document weather conditions, the menu cooked and keep a deer tally of who shot what, where and when. I've found that over the years as the stories become mingled, a quick reference to the journal keeps everyone straight as to what actually happened.

Our hunting camp has the third generation coming up through the ranks, passing on styles and techniques over the years. We've actually lost two men, who were brothers, to heart attacks while they were hunting. The second died 15 years later within a mile from where the first had died. They were our fathers, brothers or uncles, and walking through those woods makes it feel like hallowed ground. There is nothing quite like the feeling of coming to the hunting camp knowing your father won't be there with you this time. I watch over the years as each guy has to face that reality sooner

of later; it makes you realize what father and son teach each other.

Another tradition of Phantom Road Hunters is that after a member's death we hang one of their beloved racks on the wall to commemorate them and remember that person's spirit.

Dol-Mac

Hamilton D. Mc Nichol
Oscoda, MI

It wasn't Dol-Mac when I first set foot on it 44 years ago. I was twelve and the camp, 162 acres of rolling oak ridges bordered by aspen runs and spruce stands, belonged to Doc Marshall, our family dentist. Doc invited Dad and me in for the first few days of the season. I was on stand near the edge of a noisy cedar brook and about mid-afternoon on that sunny November day, I took my first deer, a forkhorn, from the land that would one day be mine.

Six years later, my father-in-law (to be), Roger Dolphyn, and my dad, Hamilton L. McNichol bought Doc Marshall's camp when the good doctor tired of harsh Michigan winters and moved to Florida. Dol-Mac it then became and, hopefully, Dol-Mac it will always remain.

Roger and Dad are gone now and my son, Erik, ghosts the same deer runs that his grandfathers knew so well. In my youth, the bucks were everything. Hundreds of them have fallen to our hunter's guns. The best of them now adorn the homes of family members and friends.

Of late, however, while the bucks are still the reason for being there, it's the companions and memories fostered over more than four decades that beckon me back each autumn. Each twist and turn of the rutted trail that winds around the camp promises a new adventure while reflecting one from the past. Up ahead is the brush-choked ravine where that big buck made me look foolish, five years past. That's the ridge where I dropped my best trophy, a wide-racked 9-point, late in the season as he slipped past in predawn light. Jake is buried on that far point. For fourteen glorious seasons we shared an uplander's bliss. Now, once or twice each autumn, I pluck a few tail feathers from a fresh killed grouse and carefully wedge them into his grave marker, along side his weathered bell and collar. Zach, my 2-year-old springer acquired from the same breeder, may not understand this interrupting ritual, but then again, maybe he does.

It's only a piece of ground, rock, stream, soil and trees. Yet, for my father, my son, family, friends and me, it has been redemption and salvation in a tumultuous world. ♠

Greenwood Valley Ranch

Kelly Vaughn & Justin Tomasini
Huntsville, TX

There is no place on earth as captivating to us as Greenwood Valley Ranch. This family-owned ranch holds the hearts and the memories of us all. The walls of the lodge tell the tales of the hunter and the hunted. From the nights of banjo and guitar playing, to the luxury of over a dozen warm cabin rooms, this ranch is truly a beautiful place. Sunsets here distinguish themselves from any other I have ever seen. When a fresh morning sun kisses the misty breath of the river, the questions remain within me, "Is this what tranquility is?" or "Is this what God looks like?"

The pride and beauty of Greenwood Valley Ranch can only be caught in the brisk moments of each photograph. However, the experience stands tall in all our hearts.

We cordially invite you to come and see us sometime. 🌲

The Peterson Farm

Gary Hetzel
Orlando, FL
Life Member

Known simply to us as The Farm, our camp is situated on a 100-acre tract of mostly planted pines in North Florida's Hamilton County.

The land has belonged to my father-in-law's family for many years and, along with another smaller property a couple miles away on the Suwanee River, provides family and friends with quality hunting, fishing and recreation.

Healthy populations of deer, turkey and hogs frequent both properties

along with smaller numbers of quail, dove and wood ducks. There are usually some gators in one of the ponds, but if you can't find them at the farm, you can always see a few along the river. In recent years, growing numbers of coyotes have provided a new hunting opportunity.

Our newest cabin, shown in these photos, has been on the property for about the last ten years. There's no running water and the nearest electric light is about 7 miles distant, but this makes for some spectacular skies on clear nights.

Florida gun season always opens on a Saturday in November, with the following weekend being the state's two-day antlerless season, so vacations are set and plans made for at least a 9-day stay in camp.

Empty milk jugs have been filled with water for the last few months, rifles have been sighted-in, lamps cleaned and filled, and supply lists drawn up and divided. These preliminary preparations being taken care of, there's still always the question of who will hunt where. And of course the issue is never decided until the late hours of the night before opening day. For some it will be one of the permanent stands like The Penthouse or The Sawdust Pile. Others will strike out for less familiar territory because of what they've seen scouting, or maybe just on a hunch.

Whether or not any deer are hung by the end of the day, or the end of the week, we are always grateful that this place is here for us and our children and, we hope, their children too. 🌲

Nick's Cabin

Chuck Pachinger
Westlake, OH

Located in Garrett County, Maryland, deep in the wilds of the Appalachian Mountains and the setting for the book *Forty-Four Years of the Life of a Hunter*, by Meschach Browning, published in 1859, stands a log cabin beside a waterfall. Just called "The Cabin" it was built in the 1920s by John E. "Nick" Herman, my grandfather and hunting partner for 20 years. The cabin once sat upon 200 acres of the wildest, most beautiful land God ever created on the Middle Fork River.

The history of Middle Fork is really quite interesting. My grandfather bought property on Middle Fork in the late 1920s. It was close to the "Old Home Place" his father had built and where my grandfather was born and raised with 14 other kids. You can still see the foundation, and the spring is still cold and sweet. Nick built a one-room cabin where Toms Spring Run runs into Middle Fork. My grandfather and grandmother cut timber up there

with a 2-man saw trying to make extra money. But it wasn't enough, and during the depression of the 1930s, the property was lost due to back taxes. They were able to purchase property below the road on Crab Tree, so they loaded the cabin up on a borrowed truck and took it there. And that's where the cabin sits today by a waterfall. And as it turns out, the man who bought Middle Fork ended up selling it back to my grandfather. So the 200 acres on Middle Fork are back in the family.

The cabin has been hunting camp for as long as I can remember: squirrel hunting, turkey hunting, and most of all deer hunting. My grandfather lived for deer season and turkey season. He knew all the deer crossings and taught them to me and all the others who hunted with him. His "deer gang" included Greg, Tony, Harold, Bobby, Donny, Jeff and Scott. We all grew up hunting with Nick and learning from him. We hunt places with names that go back to people and things from a different time: Meadow Mountain, Back Bone Mountain, Big Savage Mountain, Grass Lick Slips, Bell's Mill, Double Lick, the Humps, the Chimneys, Sugar Hill, Prop Pile, Bear Wallow, Scabby, Fox Trap, Arab's North and Jericho. We still put watchers on crossings where you can point to the "H" on a tree that Nick marked and where he probably killed a deer.

The hunters still sit and talk fondly, while waiting to start a drive, about some time or event they remember from a day when they were hunting with Nick. It might be a story about the time he stood in a hollow tree with the gun barrel sticking out of a knothole, waiting for turkeys. Maybe about the time he went out hunting with Blue, the coon dog. Blue was getting up in years but still ready to go. They left home following the train tracks down to town, picked up Greg and Tony, and went hunting on Middle Fork. Hunted all day and then went home. Blue went in and laid down by the stove and never woke up. Nick walked that dog to death. The old man was always ready to hunt. It's always a different story being told.

He passed away some years ago, but he handed down his vast knowledge and skills to us, and we are passing that knowledge and those skills to the young hunters with us today. 🌲

Vernon County A-Frame

Gerald Burke
Watertown, WI

Our camp is located in Vernon County in southwestern Wisconsin. This area is referred to as the driftless area, or that not touched by the glacier. It looks similar to Kentucky and Tennessee.

My wife and I built this A-frame ourselves, except basement and rough frame, on 65 acres of woods with 450 adjacent to hunt whitetail, turkey, grouse and squirrel on.

We built it in 1989 and have had enjoyable and successful hunting with family and friends ever since. We generally hunt all seasons with my wife, son, daughter and her husband, daughter, good friend and his wife. The small A-frame really rocks during hunting season. ▲

Camp Longshot

Scott Zarefoss
Friedens, PA
Life Member

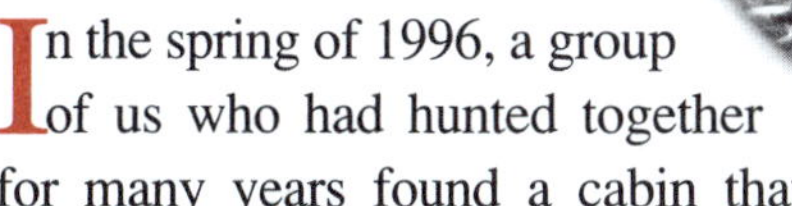

In the spring of 1996, a group of us who had hunted together for many years found a cabin that was right next to the game lands we had all been hunting on for years. The camp was kind of hidden and, although we had all driven by the driveway to the old house, we had no idea the place was there. After doing some checking with the people in the area we found out who the owner of the place was.

As it turned out the gentleman who owned the cabin had died about a year earlier and his wife didn't have any desire to use the camp, as she lived about an hour away. After a couple of phone calls, we found out that the lady was eager to get rid of the place but had never advertised it as being for sale. A couple of us drove up to meet the owner of the property and immediately were offered the property at a very reasonable price. Things were going too smoothly. On the way home, one of the guys said something to the effect that things were going too well for our bunch and that it would be a real "longshot" if we ended up getting this place.

Well the rest is history, and Camp Longshot was established. We couldn't have asked for anything better. The house is big enough to hold all 11 of us, and the property borders about 6,000 acres of game lands in Somerset County, Pennsylvania.

We spent most of the summer fixing up the old house and now the place is probably nicer than most of our own homes. The members include Don, Scott and Doug Zarefoss; Karl, Michael and Jason Bowser; Bob and Bill Snyder; Eric Kicher; Kevin Carmean; and Doug Troy. In the short period of time we've had the camp, it's been very enjoyable for all of us and our families. Not only has the hunting been great, but the close knit group of people involved make it even more enjoyable for all of us.

What started out as just a longshot has turned into something very special for all of us and our families, and hopefully we can pass down some of our traditions to the next generations, so they can get the same enjoyment out of our camp as we do.

Dead Dog Cabin

Mark "Sparky" Marcaletti
Fort Smith, AR

We built our camp in the heart of the western Ozark Mountains for the future of our kids. Tent camps became way too much hassle. Our total investment of $300 has been well worth a warm and dry bunk after a long day of hunting.

Even though our history is short, our memories will last forever. I could fill a book with the stories. Like the time "Elvis" shot a 5-point buck 200 yards from camp and drug it more than a mile the wrong way. Many, many

laughs through the years and no doubt a lot more to come.

We are surrounded by plenty of game and awesome beauty and great friends. Camp builders and hunters include Mark "Sparky" Marcaletti, Josh "Longshot" Marcaletti, Chris "Porkchop" Marcaletti, Greg "Elvis" South, Trevor "Corndogger" South, Gray "Essy" Lowe, Grant "Slim" Lowe, Lawson "Stretch" Lowe, Brian "Pinhead" Barham, and Talor "Guitar" Barham. 🌲

Sunrise Lake Deer Camp

Christopher W. Flemming
Plymouth, MN

I have to thank my Dad for lighting the fire burning deep inside me. Every man should have a passion. Mine is Deer Camp. Rumor has it that Dad warmed my baby bottles on a sterno stove when he started to take me hunting with him after I was born in 1953. In 1959 or 1960, we were partridge hunting in the Spider Lake area north of Grand Rapids when a doe jumped out in front of the car and trotted down an old tote road. We decided to follow and take the opportunity to walk the trail for birds and scout for deer sign. Like the explorers who came before us, we knew we were on to something special. From the sighting of that little doe came a love affair of a country that has held us captive for nearly 40 years. This is our story. I would like to share our deer camp memories with you.

Deer Camp: the place where men become boys and boys become men.

Deer Camp Construction

Although my dad and I hunted partridge every fall in the Spider Lake, Trout Lake and Wabana Lake area, it was not until 1965 that I started deer hunting. I had turned 12 that fall. We did not have an established deer camp at that time. In 1965, Dad had obtained a county lease on a small lake surrounded by the Chippewa National Forest. It was not until 1974 that we put up a small cabin. Until then, we stayed at the Best Western in Grand Rapids. This was our routine for several years.

Building that cabin was quite an endeavor. Without the advantage of electricity, the entire cabin was built using a hand saw and chain saw. Holes were drilled using an old brace and bit. Originally intended to be a plywood shell to keep elements out during our hunting expeditions, the interior evolved over time. Tongue-and-groove knotty cedar paneling was added along with carpeting, sofas, chairs and other amenities. We even brought in a 12-inch black and white television for Monday night football games. Without electricity and plumbing, we rely on Coleman lanterns for light and the old-fashioned outhouse for, ah, well, reading.

One feels a tremendous amount of pride in creating something with his own hands. Maybe that's why we love the place so much. The wonderful thing about Deer Camp is that it can be anything you want it to be, anywhere you want it to be.

The Week Before Deer Camp

*It was the week before deer camp
and all through the house
reigned chaos and anxiety
that no human could douse.*

*The children were hiding under their beds,
while I ran around, losing my head.
My wife thought, "what nonsense,"
as I raced down the hall;
why should the family put up with
this neurosis I catch every fall?*

*The boxes soon arrived from Cabela's and Bean,
stuffed full of equipment I knew I would need:
A parka, a hat, a new grunt call and more,
boot socks, a knife, deer scent galore.
"What did this junk cost," my wife hysterically demands?
"Why three hats, two guns and a brand new treestand?"*

*Deer camp menu is planned, only royal fare here,
partridge in cream, steak medium rare.
No canned foods for us, no green eggs and ham,
we will eat like the kings, not live off the land.
Manhattans at five, topped off with* hors d'oeuvres,
followed by the main course, then a tasty dessert.

*These last days at work, I could barely endure.
It must be Deer Camp fever, for which there's only one cure.
Each year I get older, it is more of the same,
my wife calls it folly; it's what keeps me sane.
I am indeed fortunate to be making this hunt,
now I'm off for a great time—maybe a buck.*

*It's been a long week; the stress is beginning to tell,
as the family gathers, to bid me farewell.
They had grounds to commit me to the state hospital or jail,
where there was no hope for parole, no way to make bail.
But Friday does come, and as I load up the truck,
there will be peace in the family as they wish me good luck.*

The night before opener at Deer Camp is a lot like Christmas Eve. The family gathers, plans are made for the following day. There is the electricity of excitement and anticipation in the air. The spirit is contagious, affecting both young and old. The same applies to Deer Camp Eve. The group gathers. Plans are made for the next day's hunt. Memories of deer camps past are relived and revisited. Even the most grizzled old veteran, like the young, first-time hunter, spends a restless night, waking hours before dawn in anticipation of the glorious day to come.

Deer Camp Cuisine

Our favorite part of Deer Camp is the food. After the memories of Deer Camp have faded, there remains the visions of great meals. Fried steak, partridge and wild rice, corned beef cabbage, prime rib, rack of lamb, short ribs … the list of gourmet fare goes on and on. A typical Deer Camp evening starts with happy hour, usually C.C. Manhattans and *hors d'oeuvres*, followed by a great dinner.

In addition to my love of deer hunting, I inherited my dad's talent for cooking. Like father, like son; my own son has also become an accomplished camp cook. The menu for deer camp is planned as carefully as a military campaign.

One of my Deer Camp favorites is homemade pizza. Ingredients include homemade sauce, Italian sausage, pepperoni, onion, mushrooms, Parmesan and mozzarella cheese.

Deer Camp Menu Plan

Day	Menu	Beverage
Friday	Swiss steak roasted garlic mashed potatoes	Cabernet Sauvignon
Saturday	Partridge in Parmesan and cream wild rice	Chardonnay
Sunday	Filet mignon hash brown potatoes	Merlot
Monday	Chili dogs, beef nachos Monday night football	Beer
Tuesday	Spaghetti and meatballs	Merlot
Wednesday	Sesame chicken, rice	Chardonnay
Thursday	Baked Spam baked beans	Cabernet Sauvignon
Friday	Homemade sausage and pepperoni pizza	Beer
Saturday	Chef's choice, whatever is left	Wine or beer

Memories

On November 10, 1975, the ore freighter Edmund Fitzgerald sank during a terrible blizzard that was wreaking havoc across the Northland. I remember that night so well. It was our last night at camp. Outside the cabin, the wind was howling like a freight train racing through the trees. Freezing ice and snow pelted the cabin. It was not a night to be venturing out. However, inside the cabin, Dad and I were warm and cozy. Popple "popped" in the wood stove. *Mystery Theater*, hosted by E.G. Marshal was on the battery-operated radio.

The next morning, we awoke to a snow-covered winterscape. Wet snow clung stubbornly to tree branches. Visibility was less than ten feet, making it very difficult to hunt. That morning, I missed a fat forkhorn, standing less than 100 yards from the driveway into the cabin. He was the only deer we had seen in the shortened five day season of 1975. At lunch, while listening to the radio, we heard the news about the Fitzgerald. Icy shivers enveloped my entire body as I envisioned the scene from the past night. The roar of the wind and the mountainous waves plunging the ship and its crew into the dark abyss. Such a tragedy.

Snow storms and blizzards are a common occurrence during Deer Camp. Quite frankly, I look forward to them. However, when they do occur, I can't help but go back to that fateful night of November 10, 1975, when 29 men lost their lives.

Sunrises

I love the dawn. If for no other reason than for the peace and solitude it brings to my soul. During the predawn darkness, the world is mine and no one else's. I imagine what it must have been like during the days of the voyageur and mountain man, ready to start the day's journey. For just a brief time, I walk with them, following their footsteps in the early-November snow.

With the dawn comes the thundering silence, the invigorating aroma of earth, timber and the damp fragrance of decaying leaves. And then there are colors, the awesome colors, heralding in a new day, a new beginning.

The Icing on the Cake

In our family, Deer Camp has always meant more than just shooting a deer. Of course, that is the primary objective of the endeavor. However, if that were the only objective, those lean years when the meatpole was void of venison would probably have prevented the creation of any meaningful camp tradition. I pity the hunters who have no roots and plan their season by deer numbers and doe permit quota areas. Deer Camp is so much more for us. The planning, the sights, the sounds, the food, the bonding of father and son. These are the things that keep us coming back to this special place year after year. Getting that deer is just icing on the cake.

Deer Camp—the last true measure of personal freedom. Take that away from me and I become an empty shell of a man, a lifeless soul void of passion, adrift in a universe without meaning. For the dyed-in-red-wool deer hunter, Deer Camp is the beginning of a new year. During the past year, if one has endured life's trials and tribulations, shouldered heavy burdens and nearly given up hope, then Deer Camp is a safe haven, where one goes to mend, to become energized, reborn to face the world once again. If the past year has been good, rich in rewards and opportunity, then Deer Camp is a time for reflection, a time to give thanks, a time to revel in, for it will be another year until we pass this way again.

So my friends, I hope you have enjoyed a glimpse of our Deer Camp. If you love Deer Camp as much as I do, we share a special bond unknown to most. I raise my glass to you.

Here's to deer camps past, present and future! 🌲

The Shack

David S. Pearson
Washburn, WI

A small log cabin built in 1982 by Tom Lindsey, numerous friends, and me is fondly known as The Shack. The cabin sits on 40 acres in northern Wisconsin and was built by hand from aspen logs from the acreage. Gentle gas lighting, soothing wood heat and no telephones are some of its treasured weekend attributes.

The shack has become an important part of our family life. It is frequently used during the fall and is always full for November deer season. My four sons have grown up with the hunting experience around them and nature welcoming them to enjoy her bounty. The shack has become a tradition in my family—not just for hunting, but for family gatherings. My wife prepares every Thanksgiving using the primitive shack kitchen with no running water, which has fostered a bond with our ancestors.

To quote our children, "I love the shack! Let's go to the shack!" 

The Pink Cabin

Robert D. Hoyt
Bowling Green, KY

Name: The Pink Cabin. My wife selected "Florida Coral" as the color for the cabin to accent the surrounding trees/vegetation, but when it was applied to the uncured slab boards, the color turned a brilliant pink, and so the name becomes obvious.

Location: Edmonson County, Kentucky, adjacent to Mammoth Cave National Park.

Owner: Robert D. Hoyt

Property: 60 acres; mixed upland mature hardwoods of white oak, red oak, and tulip poplar; 4 acres of bottom grassland; 4,000 feet National Park boundary frontage

Wildlife: White-tailed deer, eastern turkey and squirrel

History: I purchased the property in 1979 due to limited hunter access in central Kentucky and the desire to have a place for my four young sons and their friends to play and appreciate the out-of-doors while they grew up, and to have a private, quality place to teach my sons how to hunt. The cabin was built by Robert, Louis and Mike Hoyt, February to June 1980.

People: Our hunting/camping party includes my sons Louis, Mike, Stuart and Matt, my brothers Ed (Tennessee) and Andy Hoyt (Arkansas), my friends Tom Taylor and Matt Wilkinson and me. The cabin has been memorialized to a dear friend, Dr. Larry N. Gleason, who worked tirelessly through the '80s helping to develop the property and who was the center figure in our group. Dr. Gleason died suddenly from diabetes-complicated coronary failure in 1993.

Cabin: Dimensions are 16' x 32' with a 10' x 16' deck; built from recycled

framing joists and studs and metal roofing; exterior walls are of rough cut slab hardwood boards hung in rustic style; interior walls are of gypsum board/paneling and the floors are carpeted. The front yard has a circular drive lined on the interior with yucca plants. Horseshoe pits are centered in the middle of the front yard. The back yard slopes away from the large deck which looks out over the game pole and the valley and stream behind the cabin.

Sleeping quarters: Sleeps eight with two double bunks and two double beds; extra guests are accommodated with folding cots.

Utilities: The cabin is wired for generator electrical power; restroom facilities are external; water has to be brought in; heat is provided by a wood burning stove.

Traditions: The 1998 hunting season was the 20th year we have hunted the property and the 19th we have stayed in the cabin. To date, we have tagged 61 deer and 5 turkey on the property.

Our party gets together three times each year for 3-day hunts; spring turkey season in April, early muzzleloader deer hunting in October and rifle deer hunting in November.

Three of my sons and their friends have graduated from college now and my fourth son is nearing graduation. One son, an electrical engineer in Florida, returns for one of our hunts each year. My two grandsons are 8 years old and are being introduced to the cabin and hunting now and are carrying on the traditions we have established.

Our hunts include early- to mid-morning and mid-afternoon to dusk stand hunts on platform stands. Midday hours are spent visiting and throwing horseshoes in the cabin yard. 🌲

The Cabin

Fred Hungerford
Oneonta, NY

Dad and I built The Cabin in the fall of 1956. Every stick came from our property in the best deer country of Upstate New York. I was thirteen then; Dad passed away eight years later, but the traditions have been preserved now for well over forty years.

The list of venison recipes could go on forever, but the top few will always be venison stew, liver bacon and onions, spiedies, silver dollar steaks and pickled hearts. Venison jerky, of course, has always been the snack food of choice.

Our unofficial hunting club has about 15 or 20 members/hunters who do all the work of maintaining the trails and the blinds on the roughly 1000 acres that we hunt. We maintain a cabin log book, a photographic trophy and laugh board and, of course, a photographic honor board for those no longer hunting.

The few amenities include gaslights, indoor and outdoor kitchen, barbecue pit, two 100-yard firing ranges and an outhouse. The blessings are, to name a few, no electricity, no running water, no newspaper, and no telephone.

We have virtually no rules other than safety and consideration of others. For this reason The Cabin is used 12 months a year by members, families, co-workers and friends. The warmth of The Cabin is exceeded, only occasionally, by the temperature of the wood stove.

Full-Time Hunting Cabin

Dale Nicholas
Parish, NY

Our family has been full of avid sportsmen and women all our lives. Hunting all game—large and small—with bow, shotgun, rifle and muzzleloader.

Our camp started in 1993 and took 5 years of hard labor and love by my wife, our 3 sons, and me. We all share the same passion for the sport and fun of hunting.

The cabin soon turned into our full-time hunting trip in upstate New York. $12,000 and 5 years later, we moved into our cabin full time one week before the opening of the 1998 whitetail season. 🌲

The Cabin

Thomas L. Warschefsky
Williamson, MI

Deer camp in Michigan. What a tradition! In early 1988, my father, brother and I found and acquired The Cabin. It was a relatively remote property with acreage on a river with a cabin we could afford. All within reasonable driving distance!

We were excited then and still are. The Cabin is a traditional log cabin with pine ceiling boards and a fieldstone fireplace. It has central heat (a great wood burner) and a path bath (outhouse). We take water, and cook and light with gas. It was originally built in the 1950s by brothers who built a number of log cabins in the area. The original owners, some of whom we purchased from, had used it as a family getaway and hunting cabin. After 30 years, the original group was losing interest and dying off, and the next generation had only one person who consistently used it.

Last year, our 11th deer season there, we had three generations of our family at deer camp. We eat well, play cards, tell stories and do some seri-

ous whitetail hunting. There is always a bow camp in October that involves more canoeing, wood cutting and music playing than hunting. Then the gun season opener is on November 15, and there's a muzzle-loading weekend in December.

Hunting is done primarily from ground blinds of natural materials, and our "bait pile" is 25 yards from the picture window where we can watch the deer feed from our dining table. The largest deer we have taken are 8-pointers and approximately 175 pounds. We all have larger deer taken very close to our homes, but the tradition of deer camp brings us back. Our kids look forward to going as much as we do. To quote Ted Nugent, "We take our kids hunting so we don't have to hunt for our kids."

The fellowship with family and like-minded friends and the beauty and enjoyment of God's creation make deer camp a cherished tradition.

Southwest Virginia Camp

Roger C. Chriscoe
Asheboro, NC

Our deer camp, consisting of about 300 acres, is located in the foothills of southwest Virginia near a little town called Axton. The cabin is 5 years old and was built with logs cut from the mountains.

I decided a few years back that if I could grow up and relate with my two sons (Chad 13 and Tyler 9), we needed a special place to relate to; I wanted my wife to be part of this as well.

We've also introduced their friends to the great outdoors and hopefully will be able to keep them all out of trouble and away from drugs.

I've come to realize that a real "trophy" is something that you can talk about and share with good friends and a great family. 🌲

Summit West Hunting Lodge

Sam Fullerton
Manassas, VA

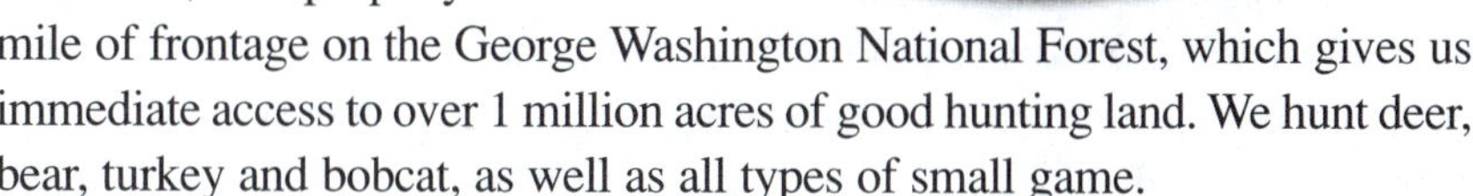

Summit West Hunting Lodge, named after my business, is located near Bergton, Virginia. Our property lies both in Virginia and West Virginia in the heart of the Blue Ridge Mountains. In addition to our own land, our property has about 1 mile of frontage on the George Washington National Forest, which gives us immediate access to over 1 million acres of good hunting land. We hunt deer, bear, turkey and bobcat, as well as all types of small game.

Opening week of rifle season in both states is a big event at our cabin with my extended family of brothers-in-law, all of our sons, some daughters, and a few special friends. It is always a time to relive old memories, tell our kids some tall tales and get excited about the upcoming hunting. We usually do pretty well, and the next big event is the photo sessions to follow the meat pole. Probably the most anticipated event to us all is our annual father/son weekend, which gives us all great quality time with our boys. Many of them have taken their first deer on this traditional hunt!

I think the consensus with all of us is that some of our most enjoyable times, as well as the most important, are those we share with our sons and daughters in a hunting camp environment; the kids are all ears and simply devour the stories told at camp. We all wish they were that attentive in school!

In addition to hunting, we spend a lot of weekends at camp through the year doing things such as tending to our wildlife food plots, cutting fire wood, maintaining treestands, scouting for next season, hiking, fishing, sledding or just simply relaxing.

189

Stannard Mountain Camp

Jeff Scott
Victor, ID
Life Member

When I was finally old enough to go to "hunting camp," it was to the one my dad and his oldest brother (Uncle Walt) had built on Stannard Mountain, which is in the heart of the Northeast Kingdom in upstate Vermont.

It was a 12' x 20' cabin with an 8' x 10' attached bunk house that was barely big enough for two people to stand up in at once. It slept 6 comfortably; however, you had to take turns walking around if there was a full attendance.

The 200 acres my uncle had was an old farmstead years earlier, but now it is covered with a large stand of hardwood trees, cedar swamps and wild apple orchards.

Later, my dad, my two older brothers Dave and Dan, and I acquired 13 acres known as the "Triangle Piece" from my uncle. With the help of a few friends (and a couple kegs of beer), we put up a 24' x 24' stick-frame build-

ing with a 16' x 24' loft that sleeps 12 people quite comfortably.

In the 20 years or so since we built the cabin, there have been countless enjoyable hours spent under that roof. And although there aren't any Boone and Crockett Club trophies on the wall, what few horns are there are trophies to all of us who are lucky enough to be able to call it our deer camp.

It's equipped with gas lights, two wood burning stoves, a large table, a couch, and a couple of easy chairs. And 'Duley' is always there on the wall to greet you with a warm smile when you walk through the door.

My brothers' sons are now old enough to go to deer camp and carry on the traditions and to hike these hardwood ridges in search of the elusive whitetail buck. My Dad turned 81 years young last year and, although he doesn't hike to the top of the mountain anymore, he still goes to camp, and with the help of his 4-wheeler can still get out to his deer stand.

I don't get to Vermont as often as I'd like to, but when I do, camp is the first place I go to. There's always a strong feeling of coming home when you walk through the door of that place ... it sure is great to be at camp!

Whitetales Bluff

Roger P. Sullivan
Ogdensburg, NY

A dozen NAHC members hunt free of charge from this 45-year-old Adirondack deer camp. The Bluff's door is open to any other club members who care to join us. Contact Roger Sullivan, 305 Cline Road, Ogdensburg, New York, 13669.

A Family Getaway

Cheryl Cleveland
Wellsboro, PA

I'm sending this in for my father, Don Monks. He and a friend of his built this cabin in 1976—then it was one room, now it has grown to three rooms and a porch; they have also brought another man in with them.

Not only is this a hunting camp, but all three families use it to get away from TV, telephone and, yes, indoor plumbing. It's like a second home to all of us.

I guess one of the best traditions there is, is going out in the winter and bowling on the frozen pond, and walking to the cemetery of the family that originally settled the land (the last member of the family died in 1899). For some reason nothing (trees or branches) ever falls in the cemetery—all around it, but never in it.

Outpost 44

William V. Griffin
Pollocksville, NC

The name of my camp is Outpost 44. The camp was given this name due to the fact that it is located so far from a public road and my CB name is 44.

The camp is three years old and is located on a part of the "Old Whitford Plantation" in my area, approximately two miles from the nearest state road. It is located on a sandy ridge in a well-drained area of mixed hardwood and pine stand of timber where one of the largest deer was harvested about 50 years ago, and it is very close to the center of the hunting area.

The camp is constructed of rough-sawed cypress lumber, stripped with cypress strips, treated with clear water sealant so it will weather and look very rustic. The interior is very rustic also. Inside the camp, in addition to the traditional deer mounts, I have hung rustic farm implements and old iron frying pans on the beams and posts made of cedar tree trunks.

The traditional hunting in this area is with "deer dogs." We also hunt from stands early in the morning and late in the afternoons. The camp is the beginning point of all hunts, whether with dogs or on stand.

We always have a big breakfast for approximately 15 to 20 hunters on each Saturday and holidays during the hunting season. The standard breakfast consists of eggs, country sausage, venison-smoked sausage, southern grits, orange juice, coffee and hot biscuits. Breakfast is a real social event. Lunch for most of the hunting days consists of venison and some type of beans.

The camp is also used for youth camp, civic groups to meet, church men's groups, conservation meeting and others. Over fifty percent of the hunters are youth under 18 years of age. It is used all year for a number of occasions. We have also had a hunting safety course taught there for youth.

Many people enjoy using Outpost 44 and that is why it was built.

Muskox Hunt Club

Terry Receveur
Collegeville, PA
Life Member

The cabin and headquarters of the Muskox Hunt Club is located off of the Wabash River on an oxbow lake in Sullivan County, Indiana. It is directly adjacent to the Club's hunting area which consists of about 3,000 acres of leased farmland and riverbottoms. The cabin and 1½ acres was purchased for $1,500 ($300 per member). The cabin is very rustic with only electricity for services (no water or indoor plumbing). It is on the inside of a flood control levee and is on stilts to keep the flood waters out.

History

The Muskox Hunt Club gained its name from an experience one of its founders (Terry Receveur) had in October of 1984. While bowhunting in Sullivan County, Indiana, he was positioned on a very heavily used trail leading through some blackberry and honeysuckle thickets when he hear the barking of some dogs coming near him. Having hunted in southwestern Indiana where wild dogs are common, he knew the dogs were probably running a deer. He readied himself for the emergence of a deer and hoped to get a decent shot. Sure enough, in less than 30 seconds a loud crashing sound was getting nearer. He looked in the direction of the noise and saw something coming toward him. At first he couldn't make it out. It was extremely large and had a very thick mane, like a lion. His first thought was, "It's a Muskox." As the thing neared, he could see that it was a monster buck with a bird's nest-tangle of vines and brush draping over its head and neck. The dogs had evidently run the buck through some pretty thick cover. He could tell the buck had a huge rack because even through all the brush he could make out long thick tines. Since that fall of 1984 we all knew the area held a monster buck and it came to be known as the "Muskox Buck."

Since the Muskox Hunt Club was formed to provide rules and regulations governing the leasing of the property where the "Muskox Buck" called home, it was decided that the club would become known as the "Muskox Hunt Club." Over the years, the hunting property has yielded some nice bucks including a 165⅝" typical shot by Tim Receveur in 1993. However, rumor has it that the "Muskox Buck" is still out there.

Membership

Membership in the Muskox Hunt Club is limited to 5 members. The founding members are Terry Receveur, Tim Receveur, Gene Shrout and Mack Collins. In 1995 the fifth member Joe Receveur (father of Terry and Tim) was added. Mack is a good friend of Joe's, who hunted quite extensively with Terry as he was growing up. Gene and Tim grew up together and have been friends since very early in school.

Traditions

The biggest tradition is simply for the reacquainting of friends and family. Terry moved away from Indiana in 1987 and has made the annual trek back for the shotgun deer hunt. Terry currently lives in Pennsylvania and the annual deer hunt may be the only trip back to Indiana he makes in a year. The reuniting with his dad, brother and good friends is a cherished tradition.

As with many deer camps, the friendly wager of $5 for the biggest buck (antler size) is something that always instigates some friendly ribbing and reminiscing. Another tradition is our Saturday night dinner. Each evening after the Saturday opener the group of five smelly hunters (remember, no running water) make the short trek into Illinois to enjoy a fried catfish dinner at a local diner.

Green Corn Dance Camp

Dominick Sacco
Newport Beach, CA

The camp is located in the Big Cypress National Preserve located in Dade and Collier County between Miami and Naples, Florida. Our relatives started hunting the area in the 1930s. The camp was rebuilt during the 1970s, and was made exempt from the acquisition program. It is one of the few surviving camps in the Florida Everglades' Big Cypress National Preserve. Due to all the controls by the park service, it is not as enjoyable as before. Our camp and land is near the "Green Corn Dance Road" which was a trail used by the Seminole Indians for their yearly festivals from 1930 through the 1970s. Travel was by canoe, walking and swamp buggies.

A lot has been lost, but we still have the memories and our yearly deer and turkey hunts. It was originally a camp with army cots covered by mosquito nets with a canvas roof between the trees—later on, a wooden shack was built. In the '70s we rebuilt the camp with a kitchen, plumbing with hot water, air conditioning, total electrical with a generator and radio communication with Miami. A lot was lost with the modern camp, and the best time was at night to turn off the generator, build a fire outside, have a drink, discuss the days hunt, look at the stars and listen to all the sounds of the swamp. 🌲

A Toast to the Season

Robert Dlugaszewski
Conshohocken, PA

In 1972, my brother asked me to go hunting with him. I had never gone before, but decided to try it. I was hooked immediately. The atmosphere at deer camp, the guys, the stories. It was just great. We hunted the same area the next year and then the bottom dropped out. The guy who had his name on the lease sold the cabin and we were left out in the cold.

In 1974, my brother and I put a down payment on a hunting cabin in Pike County, Pennsylvania. We started our own club of about 12 men. But after a few years, we wanted just a little bit more than just being there during hunting season. Along with our brother-in-law, we purchased the cabin pictured below in 1982. It was the best thing that we ever did. We spend more time there not only during buck season, but doe, archery, bear, fishing, turkey and all the off seasons. We are the same group hunting out of this cabin since 1982: my son and his 3 friends, my son-in-law, my friends, my brother's friend. My grandchildren are now talking about going hunting some day in the future. They already fish and enjoy that very much.

We only have one real tradition. On arrival at camp the day after Thanksgiving, we set up a little bar to welcome the incoming hunters. As each new hunter arrives, a toast is made to the oncoming season. No amount of money can ever buy the memories that are in that cabin and my mind. It is one of the best things I've ever done—I love it up there. Our cabin is located in Pike County, Porter Township, Pennsylvania.

Deerfoot Camp

Barry L. Moyer
Emmaus, PA

Founded in 1972 with a 50' x 10' mobile home for camp (we showered outside for 24 years). Built this log side camp in 1996. It is 28' x 32' with loft and fireplace. Living room/kitchen is a great room. Cathedral ceiling. All interior except kitchen and bath floor is 1" x 6" tongue-and-groove pine (walls and flooring).

This is a family camp: Barry L. Moyer and wife Jean who bow and rifle hunt; sons Dave and Jeff; brother Arlin and his son Chad; good friend Barry Schaedel. Some hunters also muzzle-load hunt.

Our tradition is to hold election for captain every year the day before buck season opens. This is an annual ritual with lots of fun. We also have a ceremonial circle that we gather around each morning before the hunt to wish each other good luck—the captain does the talking.

There are lots of camps with different names, but this is original. Needless to say many mounted deer feet adorn the walls along with many other trophies.

Maine Log Cabin

John W. Hogan
Rockport, MA

Located in the western mountains of Maine built in 1951 by my father Thomas L. Hogan Jr. and his father Tom Sr. and their friend Ned Cameron. Has been in use each and every hunting season since and at other times also. Constructed of pine logs cut nearby and a hand pump for water from a spring about 300 feet away. Has gas lights and an old crawford cookstove which has put out many meals and even a couple full course Thanksgiving dinners. Doesn't stay warm for long and has been pretty chilly on many mornings; the bunks are from a liberty ship which went aground off the Massachusetts coast in the 1940s.

Looking forward to this fall deer hunting season and the future for my son Jebediah Hogan. Wish we were there now!

Chester County Camp

Randy Miller
Charlotte, NC

Our deer camp is located in Chester County, South Carolina. We are very fortunate to have one of the longest deer seasons of all the states, running from September 15th to New Year's Day. Saving our vacations for hunting season, my hunting buddies and I spend at least three days a week at our camp from October through December.

Hunting deer is our main goal, but we also look forward to nights at the camp where the friendship and good food are so enjoyable. The outdoor grills are made ready, everyone cooks the food they have brought, then we all share in the feast. It is often said that we eat better at camp than we do at home. After dinner we sit around the campfire and talk about the day's events.

At 4:00 a.m. every day, we gather for the day's plans and then go off into the woods. Midday is often spent resting before the evening hunt.

Going to deer camp is a great way to escape the hustle and bustle of everyday life. Our wives often visit camp to take part in the quality time spent away from home and work.

Come the last days of December, we are saddened to think that the season is almost over. But it has again been another good season. ♣

The Red Roof Inn

David and Carol Culp
Benton, KY

We built our cabin, "The Red Roof Inn," (named by my wife), on our farm near Marion, Kentucky. It's about 50 miles from where we live. It started out to be just a place to go during deer season, but ended up being a place for my family and I to go anytime and just get away. We try to get up there about twice a month. We enjoy just sitting by the wood stove relaxing and not being bothered by the phone. We also enjoy a lot of hunting.

Camp Paradise

Jack and Flo Derouin, Eau Claire, WI
JD, Dawn and Austin Derouin, Rogers, MN
Michelle Derouin, Minneapolis, MN
Phil Derouin, Eau Claire, WI

Our family deer camp is located in the northwoods of Wisconsin. It is 20 miles from Lake Superior and is used for deer and bear hunting. We built our cabin in 1990. It was built by the members of our family with some help from a couple friends and relatives.

We also use the cabin as a summer retreat as we love to canoe the Brule River. At least once a year, we try to have a family outing which includes a trip down the river. In the spring, we cut wood for fall and winter heat and cooking, while in late summer we pick blackberries. During the hunting season, Mom cooks; Dad and the boys hunt. We've enjoyed Thanksgiving at the cabin the past 9 years; the turkey cooked in the wood cookstove is wonderful.

Family Adventure in Trempealeau County

Bill Hintzsche
Lindenwood, IL

We set up camp in Trempealeau County, Wisconsin, for the first time in 1996. We have had three successful years and hope to return for many more. It has been a family adventure, with three generations hunting together. Granddad, Charlie Hintzsche, leads the way, his sons Bill and Tim join in the adventure, while Bill's son Eric is getting off to a very good start as a young whitetail hunter. The best part about camp is enjoying the time together and the tales that ensue, after hours, around the fire.

The Swamp Hunters' Club

William Rasche Jr.
Taneytown, MD

Our hunting camp really got started in 1946. It took place in the far western part of Maryland, in and around a little town called Grantsville. In the early years, a motel room was known as "camp." The hunters consisted of brothers and brothers-in-law. Richard Cole, Raymond Cole, Roy Cole, Bud Haines, Tom Haines, Chick Haines and Claude Bohn made up the hunting party. These hunters were the forefathers of our hunting club and of the present-day hunters known as the Swamp Hunters' Club.

In 1950, they decided to start hunting from a real camp. A World War II tent was brought in with some personal gear. For the next three years, all gear and supplies were carried in on their backs approximately 1½ miles. In 1952

or 1953, Bud Haines bought a 1946 Willy's army jeep, along with a home-made trailer. An old tin stove kept the tent warm, and tables were made from tree limbs. No one had a chain saw, so all firewood was cut with a cross saw and an ax. In those early years, a few deer were killed each year—bucks only. The law then required bucks to have at least two points to one side. Spike deer were illegal. In 1958, Maryland made it legal to kill a spike.

In 1959, Claude Bohn's son, Doug, started to hunt at the age of eleven. In 1960, Doug killed his first deer, a 5-point, along with three other deer that year.

In the 1960s, several other jeeps were bought and better camping gear was bought to make camping a little easier. Many bucks were killed by both the hunters as well as friends who were invited along to hunt.

In 1970, a brand-new tent was bought. The wall tent measured 14' x 16'—large enough to accommodated more hunters. The club now consisted of ten to fourteen hunters. In 1973, some of the hunters started to bowhunt. In 1975 to 1977, Bill Rasche, Tom Rasche, Dale Blumenour and Tim Cole joined our club as members. They were greatly needed to keep our club strong, for at this time in the late 1970s and early 1980s many of the older hunters in the club, due to age and health, no longer hunted with the club, but they have never forgotten the old memories.

In 1978, Tom Rasche took his first buck, and in early 1980 Tim Cole shot his first buck. Tim is the son of early years' member Richard Cole.

Throughout the 1980s and into the 1990s many bucks have been killed. Also, we now hunt with muzzleloaders and bows. In 1996, Chad Bohn killed his first buck, a very nice 9-point. Chad is the grandson of early years' member, Claude Bohn and the son of current member Doug Bohn. Chad is the third generation to hunt in this club, along with Chick Haines's son and grandson. Tim Cole is the second generation to hunt, and his son may soon be the third generation to the camp. Tom Rasche also has two sons that we hope will become hunters.

In the '90s we now hunt from campers instead of a tent. Throughout the years of our camp, we all have become close friends. We have the greatest respect for each other, along with respect of nature and, most of all, the deer we have hunted. Although some of the names have changed, Claude Bohn, Chad Bohn, Tim Cole, Bill Rasche, Tom Rasche, Jay Wagerman, Dale Blumenour, John Rasche and Paul Haines make up our hunting camp roll call. Our camp has a great history of 53 years. As far as anyone can recall, approximately 173 bucks have been harvested, along with 19 bucks and does harvested with bows and muzzleloaders.

This is a brief history of how our camp began and how it continues today. We hope that it continues to create stories and memories.

Blanco County Deer Camp

Herb Packard
Crosby, TX

Our deer camp is located in Blanco County, Texas. It is in an area of the state known as the hill country. Our deer camp is an old stone cabin with a tin roof. This cabin has a large rock fireplace in one room. The ranch we deer hunt on is 2,000 acres.

One tradition is that we have a larger supper the night before opening day. There are ten members of our deer camp, not counting wives and children. I have been a member of this deer camp for 22 years. Even as the years pass, I still look forward in anticipation each journey to our deer camp.

Boys Deer Club

John McGoogan
Junction City, AR

The name of our deer camp is Boys Deer Club. We started it 33 years ago when some of us were teenagers. There was a deer club in our community that had mostly older men in it. Boys Deer Club is a family-oriented club where several of our wives and children hunt with us and the women kill about as many deer as the men. We have 25 members in the club and the men took turns cooking until 2 years ago when we hired a member's wife to cook for the first week of season.

Our club is in South Arkansas about 2 miles from Louisiana. We are in Tree Creeks, Arkansas, about 18 miles south of El Dorado, Arkansas. We

lease land from timber companies and private landowners to hunt on, and we also own part of the land we hunt. We had a clubhouse built from an old house until 4 years ago when we members built a new clubhouse.

We do not hunt on Sundays because we were raised to attend church and most of us are members of the church in our community.

In 1998, Arkansas passed a 3-point rule, but even so we had one of our better hunts that season.

Boys Deer Club has only had two rules all these years and they are: 1) No loaded guns in club 2) No alcohol.

We are proud of our club and our members and have a great time of hunting and fellowship each deer season.

Camp Rewipe

Lane "Bodangles" Stetler
Stevenson, WA
Life Member

I would like to tell you a little bit about our camp. Our camp's name is Camp Rewipe and we are well-known around the country where we hunt. I'll start by introducing the rest of the crew: Sniffles, Rewipe (our founder), Gramma Rambo, Buttons, Hammic, Big R and me, Bodangles. I know they seem to be awfully colorful nicknames, but believe me, every one of us has earned those names in one of our wild hunting adventures. Rewipe and I have hunted off and on for about 15 years with both of us hunting with other people as well. It wasn't until around 1994 that we started camping together with everybody else. Buttons and Gramma Rambo are my mom and dad, Sniffles is my son who has been with us for the last couple of years and Big R and Hammic are my good friends.

It is our love of archery hunting that brought us all together; we count the days until our September deer and elk hunt, and we also travel out of state to Idaho for mule deer and elk hunting. Someday in the future, we would like to go to Alaska and several other states to hunt.

Rewipe, Big R and I are NAHC Life Members, and my son is now a member. I enjoy reading your book and being a member, and someday would like to go east and hunt whitetails; I don't mean to knock anybody's style of hunting, but treestand hunting sure sounds boring. We hunt northwest blacktails in Washington, which is our home state, and they give you a run for your money. Rewipe and I were very fortunate to have dads who got us into our way of hunting; I now have the pleasure of passing along to my son the fun and adventure of bowhunting. There is no other camp that hunts as hard as we do. We hunt from dark to dark sometimes hiking as much as 12 miles or more and it's worth it. To us that is the hunt—hiking and stalking and just getting in close to the animals.

We are ethical hunters and never forget how important the woods and wildlife are to us—always leaving our camp spot cleaner then when we came.

Every year, we have a get together with our fellow rivals, Camp Back Wash, and boy do we have fun. It's a night of fun and bragging about everyone's animals.

Rewipe came up with an idea several years ago about having a hunting club and, instead of getting in trouble with our wives every year about needing money, we opened our own bank account and we all make payments every month. When it's time to go hunting, we have plenty of money for everything. Our camp consists of a 15' x 18' hunter's tent with a 10' porch where we cook. We have a wood stove for heat and are currently working on a home-built shower.

We have all harvested some nice animals, including my son Sniffles, who took his first 3 x 4 mule deer in Idaho on his first trip. I'm still looking for my first buck, but I was lucky enough to bag a nice cow on the Boise River. I also was lucky enough to take a bobcat with my bow in Washington a few years back. Rewipe took a 7 x 7 bull elk in Washington and made it into the Pope and Young Club record book in 1997, adding to his list of several bulls.

To conclude, I would like to tell all other hunters to keep up a good image about us hunters. We are a dying breed, and the better we can teach people and make them aware of our heritage, the better our chances are of surviving.

Leach Cabin—Jack County, Texas

Brian Sandleback
Coppell, TX

The Leach property is located in Jack County just west of Jacksboro in north central Texas. It has been in the family since 1896. The terrain has rolling hills with thick stands of postoak, plum thickets and pecan trees. The acorns, plums, pecans and blackberries provide a wide variety of browse for deer, turkey and other wildlife.

The original cabin was built in 1970. The expansion, as seen today, was completed in 1989. Current plans are to add a new bedroom and bath.

Several first-time hunters have taken their first deer on the property, including a fourth generation hunter in the Leach family. The hunting camp has also become a favorite spot for numerous picnics and family gatherings.

Brian Sandleback has been a North American Hunting Club member since 1994. He and hunting partner Roy Leach continue to improve the cabin and have implemented a successful deer management program for the past ten years.

South Texas Family Deer Camp

Marcus C. Canales
Rio Grande City, TX

Along with my wife Carmen and our children, whom I love very much, we would like to tell you about our family deer camp. It is a fifty-acre ranch located in Duval County way down in South Texas. My father, Arturo "Blue" Canales Jr. and my mother, Hortencia P. Canales originally purchased the ranch close to twenty years ago.

My father passed away on September 12, 1996, but I never stop missing him. I still remember the time he, my uncle Luz Gonzales and I put up the deer blind. That was years ago and it is still in the same position along with the same tie-downs as my father twisted and braced them. I'll never forget all that my father taught me about shooting rifles and hunting deer. I have a 2-year-old son and I hope I can instill some pleasant memories of hunting in him one day. A special thank you and I love you to my sister, Vilma A. Canales, who has always been a gentle, wonderful, understanding soul. And as my father watches down on us I would like to say to him, "Thank you for everything and I love you always."

Sometimes I think my father had something to do with the trophy-caliber 11-point buck I took on Christmas day in 1997. Who says you need big acreage to kill deer? I killed mine on a 50-acre spread! Having a drinking pond and feeding year 'round are a big advantage, though. Our ranch can also boast of great turkey hunting in the spring season. 🌲

Phillips Hunting Lodge

R. Larry Phillips
Midland, GA

These photographs and draw-ings show the physical qual-ities of our hunting lodge and how over the years we have collected many treasures to display, but these pieces of paper cannot tell you the family history and tradition that is so richly ingrained in our lodge.

My father, E.C. Phillips, the first of thirteen children, passed away in 1990, leaving behind my mother, two sisters and one brother. He taught my brother, Robert, and me to love the outdoors and to respect the animals we began to hunt at a very early age. We hunted in northeast Muscogee county from Pierce Chapel Road to north of Grey Rock Road on property owned or controlled by the Woodruff family. We began hunting in this area in the late 1940s, and I have some of the happiest memories of my early childhood spending this quality time with Robert and Dad.

I have so many wonderful hunting stories of great fellowship with my father, brother and uncles; however, to conserve space here, I will save these great tales for the warmth and comfort of our lodge where they take on special meaning.

In 1987, my wife Patsy and I bought a small tract of land on the backside of a subdivision being developed north of Pierce Chapel Road. Part of our property includes a beaver pond that is a great place to observe wildlife, but most importantly, it is on the property that my family and I had hunted so long ago. We built our hunting lodge in 1987 overlooking a wooded area just south of the beaver pond and within sight of where I took a bobcat that our rabbit hound "Cork" had tracked. This was when I was 13 years old (in 1956), and the photo (next page) shows how proud I was, but also that my dad shared my enthusiasm by getting the news in our *Columbus Ledger Enquirer*.

The author at age 13 with his bobcat trophy, 1956.

Today, with the City of Colombus, Georgia, ever expanding, we have moved our hunting to leased land that is only twenty minutes from the lodge.

A typical day at the lodge may include great deer or elk chili served to 20 hungry family members and friends who came in for lunch. It is not unusual to have two or three deer hanging in our processing area. We cut and wrap our meat and have a freezer handy to receive it. We have family from Charlotte, North Carolina, Atlanta, Georgia, and Tampa, Florida, who come to enjoy the comfortable sleeping accommodations provided, while enjoying the great Georgia outdoors during the day.

The purpose and mission of our lodge is to provide a comfortable place for family and friends to fellowship and enjoy the tradition of hunting. We now have a fourth generation "hunter" who has just completed his fourth season of hunting; he finished the deer season with the kill of an 8-point buck with his grandfather's

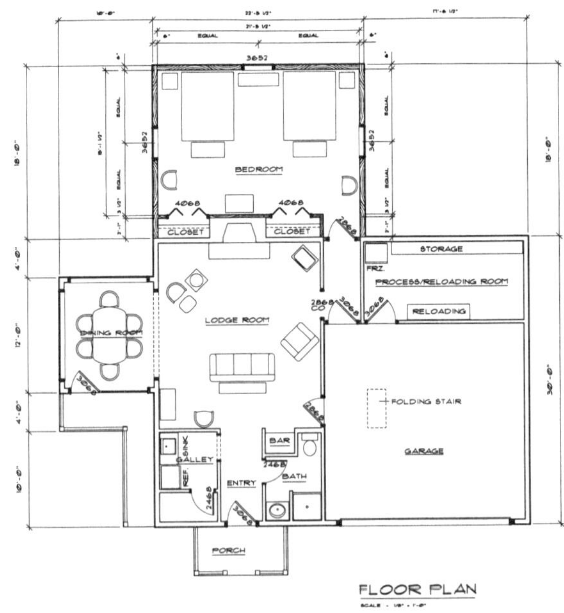

1997-98 Annual Opening Day Cookout
Phillips Hunting Lodge
"You Kill it - We Grill it!"

Opening Day Specials
October 25, 1997
Beginning at 12:00 Noon
Crock Pot Elk Stew - Spud Salad
Grilled Elk Steak - Baked

"Where eating food is more fun if you kill it with your own gun!"

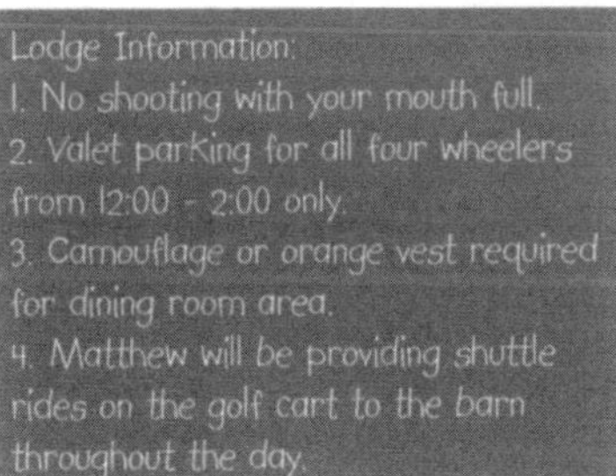

.30-30 Winchester. This was my grandson, Matthew, who celebrated his sixth birthday on September 25, 1998. I hope to instill the love of outdoors in him as my father, brother and uncles did for me. I think we are off to a great start! 🌲